Insider's Guide to SEO

Insider's Guide to SEO

How to Get Your Website to the Top of the Search Engines

by Andreas Ramos and Stephanie Cota

Jain Publishing Company
Fremont, California

Jain Publishing Company, Inc. is a diversified publisher of college text-books, professional and scholarly references, and books for the general reader. A complete, up to date listing of all the books, with cover images, descriptions, review excerpts, specifications and prices is always available on-line at **jainpub.com**.

Limits of Liability and Disclaimer of Warranty

Trademarks

Copyright Notice

Printed in USA

ISBN 0-87573-051-5

Table of Contents

Preface

This book discusses search engine optimization (SEO) and how to optimize webpages to improve their ranking in the search engines. This book explains the logarithmic nature of the web and network theory. By understanding search engine technology and the web, you can develop a better strategy that will improve your webpage positions in search engines.

- Search engine optimization is a short-term tactic.
- Paying for search engine placement is a quick solution with immediate results, but it is also a short-term tactic.
- The best strategy is to develop informational content. Your webpages will be ranked higher and stay there.

Audience

This book is for marketing departments and webmasters who supervise an ecommerce website. This can also be used for non-profits and other groups that use websites to reach a large audience.

To implement the technical SEO, you'll need to know a bit of HTML. You can also just hand the chapter to your webmaster.

About the Authors

Andreas Ramos has worked for a number of Silicon Valley companies. He wrote one of the first books on web design and managed ecommerce sites for years. He was the webmaster for a company that grew at over one million users per month for more than a year. Andreas lives in Palo Alto with his cat. Visit him at andreas.com.

Stephanie Cota's clients include a number of Silicon Valley startups. She built a web-based enterprise system for the State of Nevada. She wrote an entire ecommerce engine from scratch, including secure online credit card transaction, invoicing, merchant tools, inventory control, and shipping fulfillment. Stephanie also lives in Palo Alto. Visit her at stephaniecota.com.

Andreas and Stephanie have spoken on technology issues in New York, Los Angeles, San Francisco, Palo Alto, Chicago, Minneapolis, Albuquerque, Vienna, and other cities.

They build and manage ecommerce websites. This includes automated tools, interactive databases, and other tools and technologies, many of which they've developed themselves. For more, visit their website at CreativeConsultantsGroup.com.

Acknowledgements

Special thanks to: Ginger Lee (Silicon Valley marketing), Thomas Wong (ecommerce expert), Emily Berk (webmaster), Dida Kurz (manages her own ecommerce site), Darrell Newcomb (network architect), IdaRose Sylvester (Silicon Valley marketing), and Charles Jo of Inteliant Technologies (one of Silicon Valley's top recruiters). They read the manuscript and made valuable suggestions. Hedwig Ronronne and Eurydice Katzenjammer also made contributions.

Laura Wood, a web developer who manages a number of ecommerce sites and AdWord accounts, shared many ideas and tips.

Disclaimers

Andreas and Stephanie manage the SEO work for a number of companies. Andreas once worked for an SEO company. The authors are not affiliated with any search engine or SEO company. None of the examples in this book is based on these companies. Any similarity is coincidental.

The Illustrations

The illustrations for this book come from advertising images from the 1920s to the 1940s. This was a period of innovation in marketing and art deco illustration. The images are available from Dover Publications.

The book cover layout is by Lisa Cardoza in San Francisco.

The book layout is by Eurydice Katzenjammer.

The Koi Website

The book uses a fictitious website as an example. Koi-Heaven.com sells koi, a type of goldfish. There is no Koi-Heaven.com.

Updates and Feedback

For updates to this book, or to give feedback, visit the website for this book at CreativeConsultantsGroup.com/seo

Notes and Tips

 Note: Pointer Dog tells you about notes or additional information. For all of the notes, see the index.

 Tip: Betty tells you tips and helpful hints. If you want to see all of the tips, there's a complete list in the index.

Clickable Links in this Book

For a list of clickable links, go to CreativeConsultantsGroup.com/seo

Insider's Guide to SEO

Introduction

In this Chapter

What is SEO? Here's the short answer: SEO is Search Engine Optimization. It's how you modify websites so that they rank higher in search engines.

So how do you do this? "How do I SEO my website?" someone once asked a Google speaker at a search engine conference. The reply was "write good content". What did Google mean by that? This book explains the answer.

The Search Engines' War against SEO

SEO is a collection of methods to getting a website to rank higher in a search engine. But search engines don't like SEO. They go out of their way to counter the SEO strategies.

To understand why search engines don't like SEO, we have to look at the conflict between search engines and spammers. This will lead you into the world of search engines.

Okay, you're selling koi, a type of decorative goldfish for collectors. You want your website Koi-Heaven.com to be listed #1 in your category for koi fish in the search engine results.

But let's be honest here. In your deepest fantasies, you want to be #1 not just in your category; you want to be #1 in every single category in the search engines. When people search for Hawaii vacations, golf clubs, whatever: you want Koi-Heaven.com to be the first item on every list. And why just #1? How about the first 100 positions for every single search? That'd really sell quite a few koi.

This isn't a far-fetched idea. The spammer websites try to do this.

- Back when search engines used meta-keyword tags to index a page, the spammer websites found they could put Britney Spears, Disney, Porsche, and other top keywords in their webpage meta keywords. When people searched for those words, they were brought to the spammer site. By inserting misleading keywords, it was easy to get the number one spot in categories where the site didn't belong. Many top positions in search engines were spammer sites.

- Webmasters also realized that they could repeat the keywords in the meta-keyword tag and their webpage would appear at the top of the list.

That was an early example of SEO. By misusing the meta-keyword tag, the spammers were able to mislead the search engines. That's why nearly all of the major search engines have stopped using the meta-keyword tag.

The point of SEO is to get YOUR webpage to rank higher than other webpages, regardless of the quality of your webpages. To put it another way, SEO is basically the art of fooling search engines. That's why search engines don't like SEO.

Commercial websites can afford to pay for advertising. Why should the search engines care if companies buy the top 100 spots? Why not just sell the top 100 spots to companies?

Insider's Guide to SEO

This is the other side of the equation. The large majority of users don't want to see commercial information.

- 85% of searches are for information. People are searching to learn about something.

- 11% of searches are commercial searches. People are searching for a product or service.

For a search engine to draw a large number of users, it must be able to supply links to non-commercial information. If there are too many commercial sites in the top spots, users will go to another search engine.

Some people may think that search engines are run by naïve theoreticians or academic librarians and search engines should get out of the way of commerce. If search engines didn't block SEO, your koi company would get the number one spot in every category. For about two days. And then the spammers would completely swamp the search engines and the first 100 items for every category would be porn websites.

 These numbers are based on a Pennsylvania State University study. About 11% of some 30 million daily searches at Excite are business queries. At AskJeeves, it is 6%. Other studies show the same general numbers. See a summary at firstmonday.dk/issues/issue6_7/spink

There's also the issue of companies trying to place advertising in the search engines. How do the users feel about this? What are users searching for, what do they expect to find, and how do they feel when they find commercial sites?

How Do Users Feel about Ads?

Consumers Union did a study in June 2003 to see how users perceive search engines and advertising on search engines.

First of all, the study finds that users have a naïve trust in search engines to deliver the best, unbiased information on a search. They think the pages listed at the top are also somehow the most trustworthy.

In general, users don't understand how search engines work. They don't understand how pages are ranked. They don't know that search engines are commercial enterprises. They don't realize that many search engines include paid items in the results.

When they search, they are searching for information. If they notice that links are advertising, they skip over those links. Users like it when advertising is highlighted because that lets them ignore the ads. If they are searching for information and they click on a page that turns out to be commercial, they immediately back out of it so they don't waste time.

When users find out that a search engine is placing paid links at the top of the list, they react very strongly.

- Their emotions include dismay, shock, revulsion, annoyance, anger, disgust, disappointment, and helplessness.

When users realize a search engine is inserting paid links in the results, the search engines lose credibility. Users switch to another search engine.

 The comments and attitudes in this section are in a study by Consumer WebWatch, a project of Consumers Union, the non-profit publisher of *Consumer Reports* magazine, at consumerwebwatch.org/news/searchengines/index.html.

There's still a place for commercialized search engines. If users are shopping, then they expect and accept paid links in the results. Some ecommerce web-masters put their emphasis on Yahoo!, because users tend to shop there. Amazon is developing a search engine named A9.com that lets you search and it also shows related books and products.

The search engines and users don't like manipulation of the search results. There's yet another problem for companies. The search engines are constantly changing. What's coming in search engine technology?

The Future of Search Engines

Search engines compete against each other by seeing which one offers the most relevant results. This is called relevancy, and the search engine that offers the best relevancy in their results will get the most traffic. That's worth tens of billions of dollars.

However, search engines are not very good at delivering relevant results because the current technologies aren't able to distinguish between the different meanings of the same word. For example, you search for jaguar. Do you mean Jaguar as in the cat in Brazil, the code name for the Macintosh operating system, the British car, or the Jacksonville football team? If you keep getting the wrong kind of jaguar, you'll try a different search engine.

There are several upcoming search engine technologies to improve the relevancy of results.

Context-Based Results

Search engines are trying to develop artificial intelligence software that can identify information as types of clusters and then display information based on the cluster you want. These search engines show the results in context.

Several examples of context-based search engines include Teoma.com, Mooter.com, and Kartoo.com.

When you search at Teoma, it asks you to select a cluster. If you select big cats, then it'll show only results that have to do with feline jaguars.

 In Spring 2004 Google introduced their version of context-based search. You can try this at http://labs.google.com/personalized. Set up a Personalization, do a search, and move the slider button back and forth. The results change instantly.

Customer-History Searching

Another future type of search engine is based on the customer's history of searches. This type of search engine watches the kinds of webpages you visit and when you make a new search, it offers results that match your past interests and web search habits.

For example, it notices that you look at jungle cat pages. When you finally search for jaguar, it's going to show you webpages about jaguars in South America. It will not show you webpages about Jaguar the Macintosh software, no matter how much money they spend on SEO for their website.

Either of these upcoming technologies will give the user more power to block unwanted information. Companies will not be able to influence the search engines because users will be setting their own interests.

Information Ecologies and Text Analytics

When you search at Google, you find the top websites for a topic. But this finds what other people already know. They've already written webpages about those issues. How can you find what people don't yet know? What if the data is scattered across dozens of databases and hasn't yet been recognized by humans as information? The current search engines have no way of identifying or displaying such information.

Another problem with current search engines is their literal search. They find only exactly what you search. If you search for steel frying pans, you only get pans made of steel. It won't show frying pans made of cast iron, aluminum, copper, ceramics, titanium, or anything else. Humans can recognize similarities, even when they didn't know there were frying pans made of titanium.

The next trend in search engines will be tools that can look at data and find relationships in the same way that humans can look at information and find patterns. These search engines will be able to look at general concepts and find similarities, even when you didn't know to ask for them. When you ask for steel frying pans, these search engines will show results for related types of frying pans, including titanium frying pans and other forms of kitchenware that is used for cooking.

This moves into an area called text analytics. By marking up a document with meta-information, such as general concepts, categories, classes, location, size, and more, search engines would be able to identify related information. This would include the hidden implications and assumptions that lie behind words. This allows search engines to find other terms in the same category.

One of the largest projects in text analytics is being developed by the IBM Almaden Research Center. Their project, called WebFountain, is a platform that allows other companies to develop tools to search for patterns in data spread across millions of webpages, web directories, chat lists, blogs, emails, text documents, spreadsheets, databases, weather data, and so on. IBM's WebFountain also includes Factiva's collection of 9,000 newspapers, magazines, and trade journals.

These search engines could discover patterns, trends, and relationships in the stock market, the fashion world, and so on as they happen. Companies could anticipate new patterns in consumer demand, discover new markets, or identify new rivals. Governments could plan better by looking at financial data over a five-year span to see how the economy is developing. States could look at job listings in thousands of newspapers to find emerging trends in employment and use this information to allocate funds for training.

WebFountain can be used for more than just identifying trends. Companies can use this to monitor their corporate image and message, and if negative or unwanted trends arise, the companies can change their information to improve the corporate image. This prevents the spread of negative information for a company's brand. This creates the ability for a company to have a proactive approach in managing their brand.

For example, there may be a car defect that leads to accidents. But if it rarely happens, automobile manufacturers may not know about it and automobile websites may not write about it. However, on chat lists and blogs that are not related to cars, people may mention that while driving to bring their koi to the vet, the steering wheel felt funny and they had an accident. If a search tool allows you to look for mentions of accidents that use loosely related terms, notice the dates and locations of accidents, look at the weather for those cities, check the databases of car manufacturers and steering wheel makers, and then correlate all of this together, it could discover new patterns.

Such search engines will be quite valuable tools. These go beyond the current level of consumer search. When you search on Google and similar search engines, you find only the pages that match the search terms. These pages are ranked by the number of other pages that link to them. Users generally click only on the first few results. The overall informational value of the result is quite low. A tool that can show correlations, relations, and context to discover new information would be very useful.

Summary: Search engines will change substantially in the next few years as they add search based on personal interests and develop text analytics so they can identify information trends. To be certain that your website will be found in these new search tools, the best strategy for you is to offer what search engines want to see. Search engines are interested in indexing the web and delivering the best information. If you provide good information, you will be ranked highly. This means adding lots of good information so your website will be significant within its information cluster.

How Search Engines Rank Your Website

In this Chapter

This chapter explains how search engines rank webpages. By understanding this, you'll know what to go after in your website placement strategy.

The Goal of Search Engines: Indexing and Ranking the Web

There are some six billion webpages (Spring 2004), but only a third of these are indexed. The rest are ignored.

Search engines don't index abandoned pages or trivial pages. How do the search engines know if a page is trivial? They check to see if other pages link to it. If the page has low informational value, then other people won't bother to link to it. There are some two billion trivial webpages, which is about a third of the web.

Search engines also ignore duplicate pages, redirects (pages that jump to other pages), and obsolete or abandoned pages. These make up another third of the web.

This leaves some two billion pages. Search engines use various strategies to index and rank those pages:

- Search engines categorize the web into collections of information clusters. For example, all the pages about Macintosh computers form a cluster. Pages about the Berlin Wall form another cluster.

- Search engines place webpages within those clusters according to their informational value (the quality of the information), links to the webpage within the cluster, and other criteria.

- Search engines downplay, ignore, or ban irrelevant webpages or webpages that manipulate search engines.

Summary: Search engines use informational value of a webpage and how well it fits into a cluster in order to index and rank webpages. They do not use much of what generally passes for SEO (namely, modifying the HTML code to index and rank the webpages.)

At the beginning of the web, Yahoo! indexed the web manually. They had rooms of humans who indexed webpages. However, as the web grew explosively, they couldn't keep up.

Search engines began to develop automated indexing tools. These use various rules to automatically sort webpages into categories and then rank those pages according to significance. This works fairly well, but new problems arise from the nature of the technologies.

The Mathematical Nature of the Web

To understand ranking, we have to look at how items are listed in the search engine results. You search for a topic and the search engine returns a list of webpages. What does it mean to be on the fifth page in comparison to the tenth page? What percentage of traffic goes to the first page compared to the second page? Is there a way to calculate this?

In daily life, numbers are linear: they grow according to simple addition. You drive your car at 40 mph. If you increase the speed to 50 mph, that's ten mph faster. You increase again to 60 mph, which is ten more. To understand car speeds, you only need to add or subtract numbers.

Logarithms are another kind of number. In California, we're quite familiar with log numbers. Earthquakes are measured by the Richter Scale, which is based on logarithmic numbers. A Richter 5.0 is ten times as powerful as a Richter 4.0. A Richter 6.0 is ten times more powerful than a 5.0 and 100 times more powerful than a 4.0.

By the mid 90s, physics researchers began to study the web. They quickly discovered the growth, quantity, and distribution of links on the web are based on log numbers.

For example, your webpage is on the third page at Google. If we look at three as a logarithmic number, then page one gets basically 90% of the traffic for that topic, page two gets a tenth of the traffic and page three gets 1% of the traffic. If a webpage isn't on the first three pages in a search engine, that's pretty much the same as not being there at all.

If people apply linear numbers to the web, they will seriously misunderstand what is happening. They will think that going from the page two hundred to page five is a great improvement. However, seen from a log scale, that is hardly any difference.

If we put these numbers on a linear graph, the numbers make little sense. The line creeps along at the bottom of the graph and then suddenly spikes off the chart.

However, you can graph log numbers on a log chart. This uses log numbers for the X and Y axis (horizontal and vertical). The resulting chart looks like this:

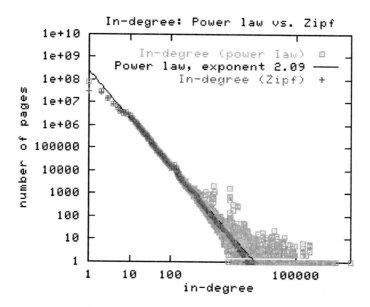

Figure 1: Example of a chart on a logarithmic scale. The X and Y axis use log scales. Log charts characteristically have a straight line instead of a curve. The chart displays the distribution of webpages that have inbound links. (Illustration from IBM Almaden Research Center.)

A few webpages are at 10^8 (at the upper left), and most webpages are clustered at the bottom (at the lower right). (In the middle of the chart, you'll notice a cluster of webpages that don't fit the line. Those are spammer pages. There are so many that they form their own cluster.)

This theory is supported by various studies of users. In the Consumers Union study (mentioned in the Introduction), 88% of the users stayed on the first page of the search engine results. 16% went on to the second page. 2% went as far as the third page. A study by Excite.com studied 200,000 users and one million searches. 70% looked at only the first two pages of results.

Another study found 97% of users clicked only the first ten links (and 71% clicked only the first five links.) In a University of Pennsylvania study, 50% of users view only the first page of results, 19% went to the second page, and 10% went to the third page of results. 55% of users looked at only the first item; 80% looked at only the first three items. As you can guess, those numbers are logarithmic distributions.

- A few webpages have lots of traffic. The vast majority of webpages get little traffic.

- There is no gradual transition or equal distribution. You get either nearly all the traffic in your category or you get crumbs.

Logarithmic distribution applies to personal webpages, corporate webpages, university webpages, and the web as a whole. It also applies to the distribution of keywords. A few keywords will get most of the traffic.

Google's PageRank Algorithm

Google uses an algorithm (a mathematical formula) to rank the webpages in its index. The Google algorithm's main idea is simple: pages are ranked by the number of links to those pages. The more links to a page, the more valuable that page is. A link to a page is a vote for that page. Someone else thought the page was significant so he added a link to that page.

However, this method also has non-obvious implications. If people vote for webpages, it seems that would rank the pages fairly evenly. The good ones would be at the top, most would be in the middle, and the bad ones end up at the bottom. However, it doesn't happen that way because the web's distribution is based on logarithms. The result is that a few pages get a disproportionate amount of the votes and most pages get very little. Thus the Google algorithm uses logarithms to rank webpages.

If you install the Google toolbar in your browser, you can see your webpage's logarithmic value. In the following illustration, open a webpage and then point to PageRank in the Google toolbar. A text box pops up and shows that the Google PageRank (PR) is 5.

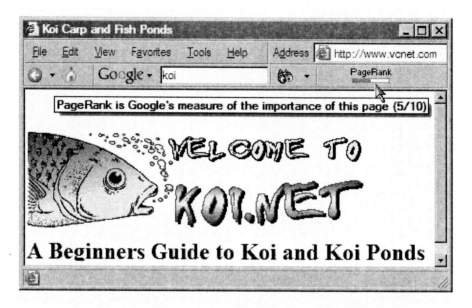

Figure 2: Point at PageRank in the Google Toolbar to see the PageRank of a webpage. In this case, Koi.Net webpage's PageRank is 5 (also called a PR5).

This PageRank number is a logarithmic value. To keep this simple, let's assume Google is using Base 10 (each log number is ten times greater than the previous number, as in the earthquake Richter Scale). This means a webpage with a PR5 value is ranked ten times higher than PR4, 100 times higher than a PR3 webpage, 1,000 times higher than a PR2 webpage, and 10,000 times higher than a PR1 webpage.

To complicate things, Google doesn't use base ten. It's a bit complex to explain base numbering systems and we won't do that. The point is that Google uses a base that is a fraction between six and seven. If it is base 6, the multiples will be six times greater for each step. PR5 would be six times greater than PR4, 36 times greater than PR3, 216 times greater than PR2, and 1,296 times greater than PR1. If it is base 7, then the steps grow by multiples of seven. Google uses a fractional base, which mean the steps grow by a number between six and seven.

To make matters yet more complicated, the Toolbar PageRank value isn't identical to the Google PageRank value. You can think of the number in the toolbar as a rounded off version. If we assume a base 6 log scale, PR5's actual value could range from 1,296 to 7,775 (that is, it can be a low PR5, a mid-range PR5, or a high PR5.)

In any case, the Google Toolbar PR value gives you an idea of a webpage's significance.

- Install the Google toolbar in your browser. It shows the page rank for webpages, both yours and your competitors. Fetch it for free at toolbar.google.com

If you know your webpage's monthly traffic, this can give you a rough idea of your competitors' traffic. If your webpage has PR5, then a competitor's page with PR4 page has a sixth to a tenth of your traffic. A PR6 page in your category will have perhaps six to ten times as much traffic. Keep in mind that the PageRank values can range within these number: there can be a low PR5 or a high PR5 value.

If you want to read more about PageRank and the Google algorithm, the original articles are at Stanford University's website.

- The Anatomy of a Large-Scale Hypertextual Web Search Engine, by Brin and Page. http://www-db.stanford.edu/~backrub/google.html

- The PageRank Citation Ranking: Bringing Order to the Web, Page, Brin, Motwani, Winograd. http://dbpubs.stanford.edu:8090/pub/1999-66

- There are number of good articles about PageRank. See Ian Roger's article at iprcom.com/papers/pagerank, Andrew Gerhart's article at searchengineguide.com/orbidex/2002/0207_orb1.html, Harjot Kaleka's article at searchguild.com/article112.html, Tony Bury's article at sitepoint.com/article/999?, and Phil Craven's article at webwork-shop.net/pagerank.html

- For more articles, see the References section at the end of this book.

 Websites or webpages? People tend to use the two terms as if they are the same thing. However, for search engines, there is no such thing as websites. They index webpages, not sites. A website could have a single highly-ranked page yet the rest of the website can be low-ranked pages.

The Landscape of the Web

Webpages can also be classified by the type of links they have. The IBM Almaden Research Center in Silicon Valley studied the link distribution in a small collection of two hundred million webpages and found that the web consists of five groups:

- 28% of webpages are the core of the web. These pages are highly cross linked among other core webpages.

- 21% of webpages lead INTO the core. These pages point to the core, but there are no links from the core to these pages.

- 21% of webpages are linked FROM the core. The core links to these pages, but the pages have no links to the core or other pages.

- 22% of webpages form a number of groups that are linked FROM the core, but these groups don't lead to other groups or the core.

- 8% of webpages are isolated islands. There are no links to or from these pages.

Why are there so many isolated webpages or pages without links to other pages? Many companies refuse to crosslink their sites. They want to trap the visitors within their site. A link allows the visitor to go away. However, this means that other sites probably won't link to these pages and these sites will have less traffic.

- You can read the IBM paper at almaden.ibm.com/cs/k53/www9.final/

Summary: To get your webpages into the core of the web, create a website that gets other webpages to link to you. You must also link to other pages.

Fluctuation in Ranking

If you watch your webpage's position at a search engine, you may notice it will change over the course of the month. It can rise and fall dramatically. At Google, this is called the Google Dance. It happens because Google is in the process of re-indexing and recalculating the PageRank for every page in its index.

Google indexes the web roughly in the last week of the month. Pages with high PR are indexed more frequently.

• The more links to your webpage, the less the fluctuation will affect you. If your ranking is based on many webpages, then changes in a few webpages won't matter so much.

Summary: This chapter explains logarithms. This is one of the basic concepts in Google's approach to indexing the web. The log scale means the webpages at the top of a category will get most of the traffic. If a webpage isn't at the top of its category, it may as well not be on the web.

Network Theory and the Web

In this Chapter

What does it mean when people say the web is a network? Let's look at the field of network theory in mathematics and physics. By understanding this, you'll know how the web grows, why the top websites grow yet faster, and how a few websites can affect the rest of the websites within their cluster.

Origins of Network Theory

In the 1780s, Euler invented the field of network theory and for most of the next two hundred years, it was a form of abstract mathematics. A network is made up of nodes and links. Nodes are the connectors; links are the connections between nodes. For example, in a social network, nodes are the people and links are the friendships between them. On the web, nodes are the webpages and links are the links between webpages.

In network theory, mathematicians assumed the links between the nodes were randomly distributed. If there are, say, 10 nodes and 50 links, they assumed each node had on average five links.

The Social World as a Network

If one applies the random distribution of networks to the social world, then six billion humans (the nodes) should each have generally the same number of friendships (the links).

However, sociologists and economists realized that real-world networks were not randomly distributed.

In the early 1900s, Vilfredo Pareto, an Italian economist, discovered the 80/20 Rule:

- 20% of landowners own 80% of the land.

- 20% of salespeople make 80% of sales.

- 20% of webpages get 80% of the traffic.

Stanley Milgram performed his famous six-degrees-of-separation experiment in the 60s. The popular understanding of Milgram's experiment is that anyone can be linked to anyone else on Earth through only six links. In fact, Milgram discovered:

- **Three Links of Separation**: Some people have such good links that they can get to someone far away through only three links.

- **100 Links of Separation**: Others require up to a hundred links to reach someone else. This also means the people within those hundred links are also poorly linked.

- **No Links**: Milgram also found that many people have such poor links that they can't establish a connection to distant others. These people live in small social networks, but they are isolated from society at large.

In the late 60s, Mark Granovetter, a sociologist now at Stanford, studied how people found jobs. Until then, it was generally assumed that society was homogenous and everyone had pretty much the same access as others. Granovetter discovered that society is made up of groups of people, which is now known as clustering. Granovetter showed that weak contacts were twice as effective (28%) as strong contacts (17%) for finding a job. Casual connections were more likely to lead to a job.

This seems counter-intuitive. It would seem close friends would be better job leads. However, we tend to gather within groups of similar interests. Sociologists call this the "birds of a feather" phenomenon, as in "birds of a feather flock together."

For example, if a tennis instructor wants new students, there's no point for her to ask her friends because they are all tennis instructors. She will find new students by asking people in social clusters outside of tennis, such as church groups, knitting clubs, and so on. Those social clusters probably lack members who are tennis instructors.

These various sociological phenomena (Paretto's 80/20 Rule, Milgram's six degrees, Granovetter's social clustering, and Zipf's laws) were known, but there was no satisfactory explanation because there was no way to quantify large social networks. You can write down a list of your friends. But this will grow very fast when you add the list of friends of friends. If you add a further circle of friends of friends of friends, the numbers become too large.

What was needed was a real-world network that could be exhaustively mapped, such as the web.

The Internet as a Network

In the mid-90s, physicists began studying the web because it was an example of a network in which all the nodes and links could be tracked. Although the Internet was originally designed to be randomly distributed, computer scientists realized there was a pattern to its distribution. Maps of the web showed that some nodes had huge numbers of links, while most nodes had only a few links.

Albert-Lazlo Barabasi, a physics researcher, discovered that computer networks use logarithmic distribution, highly-linked nodes grow faster, and networks undergo phase transitions.

- The distribution of links in a network can be measured by logarithmic numbers. A few nodes get most of the links. Most nodes have few links.

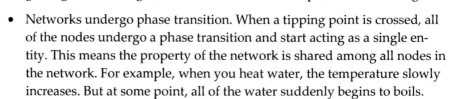

- As new nodes enter the network, they are more likely to link to highly-linked nodes than low-link nodes because the highly-linked nodes are easier to reach. This creates a feedback loop in which the largest nodes get larger. The rich get richer. Barabasi calls this "preferential linking."

- Networks undergo phase transition. When a tipping point is crossed, all of the nodes undergo a phase transition and start acting as a single entity. This means the property of the network is shared among all nodes in the network. For example, when you heat water, the temperature slowly increases. But at some point, all of the water suddenly begins to boils. There is no gradual boiling or localized boiling.

In terms of websites, logarithmic distribution means that a few websites will get the majority of the market. Due to preferential linking, the largest sites will grow yet larger. As for phase transition, there can be a number of dot-coms in a small market and at first, the various websites will be different. But when the market niche crosses a certain size, a few of the websites become very large and the remainder stay small. All of the websites take on the properties of the group. In other words, the small websites adapt the general standards of the largest websites.

Incidentally, this also shows why networks (the web, social networks, biological networks, and so on) easily survive attacks. If a computer virus spreads into a network and destroys perhaps 10% of all nodes, that's not really a problem, because 80% of nodes have low value. Losing many low-value nodes will not affect the network as a whole. However, if an attack targets the key nodes (the 20%), it can be catastrophic. The entire network may collapse.

How Search Engines Rank Webpages

Yahoo!, one of the first directories, was started by two Stanford students in their dorm room. It was a list of websites that was maintained manually. If you wanted to be added to Yahoo!, you sent a personal email to the students. That worked in the first year or so, when there were only several thousand websites.

The web soon grew to several million pages. Yahoo! hired workers to continue added sites, but soon it became obvious that the web was growing too fast to keep up and the web would soon be too large to maintain a human-edited list.

Search engines needed a way to automate the indexing and ranking of the web. This meant a computer program that could do this on its own.

A similar problem had already occurred in the early 1900s. Scientific journals were growing faster than the ability of librarians to index it.

In the 1920s, Hulme, Lotka, Gross and Gross, Bradford, and others carried out research in library science on how to evaluate articles and journals. In the early 60s, Price published two books that introduced modern bibliometrics.

The first citation analysis was carried out in 1926 by Gross and Gross (a husband and wife team), who examined 3,633 citations in the 1926 volume of the *Journal of the American Chemical Society*. They noticed that articles in chemistry journals had citations to other articles. If an article was significant, then other researchers would cite it in their research. If it wasn't significant, then it would have few citations. This meant it was possible to create a system so that non-chemists could assign the significance of an article, simply by counting how many other articles linked to it.

In the mid-90s, Sergey Brin and Lawrence Page, two computer science researchers at Stanford, wrote a computer program that used bibliometrics to analyze the value of webpages. Just as with chemistry journal articles, the Brin/Page method ranked a webpage by the number of other pages that linked to it. If a page was significant, then other people would take the effort to create a link to it. If the page was trivial, then there would be few or no links to it.

Brin and Page's software became Google. It's not the only links analysis tool and it's not necessarily the best one. It's just the best known example of computerized bibliometrics, which is also called cybermetrics.

Google's method assigns an authority value to a page. If many pages link to it, then the target page is an authority. Jon Kleinberg, a researcher with IBM, proposed that a page should have an authority value (how many pages link to it) and a hub value (how many pages it points to.) Another version of Kleinberg's algorithm ranks a webpage if it points to major authorities. If your koi webpage lists the five top koi magazines and the international and national koi associations, then the webpage has informational value. The Teoma search engine is based on Kleinberg's algorithm. There are additional methods by other researchers.

These various tools can be tested by using the same dataset, making a search, and comparing the results. Link analysis works well when the topic is clearly defined, there are significant articles about it, and it has an interconnected community of webpages. But if these assumptions aren't met, several odd problems can occur.

For example, if a group of pages are highly-interlinked within a "tight knit community" (TKC), the pages can appear to be significant (they have many links) although they have no real value. For example, several years ago a bunch of bloggers linked the words "dismal failure" to Bush's personal page at the White House. If you search for dismal failure, you got George Bush.

If the topic is vague, there aren't good webpages about it, or there aren't interconnected communities that discuss the issue, then the search engines produce wrong results. This is known as the topic drift problem (TDP). For example, search for net gain. This produces 6.8 million hits, but the results are random pages.

More Resources

You can find more on network theory at CreativeConsultantsGroup.com/seo.

 These laws about networks apply to many kinds of networks: the web, wealth and property distribution, membership on corporate boards, personal friendships, business and commerce, the growth of cities, food chains in biology, intracellular protein molecules, and so on.

The Implications of Network Theory

You can see the implications of network theory for your webpage.

- Companies that pursue a "business is war" strategy are at a self-inflicted disadvantage. They create few links, newcomers don't link to them, their websites are isolated, and so on.

- Companies that embed themselves into their information cluster by creating lots of links to other companies, suppliers, industry magazines, customers, government, and workers will grow, because the node with the most links will get more links. At some point, the network will undergo a phase transition from "just a bunch of separate companies" into an industry. The core companies become institutionalized and they own the industry. Their internal standards become the industry's standard. Pareto's 80/20 Rule applies and 20% of the companies will get 80% of the revenues. Due to the law of preferential linking, newcomers will be effectively locked out of the market space.

Summary: This chapter explains network theory. Physics researchers have shown that this theory underlies the Internet and the web and explains how it functions. Websites that pursue a strategy to establish themselves as the hubs of their category will become the major websites in those categories. Those websites will get the lion's share of traffic and revenues in their category.

Technical SEO

In this Chapter

This chapter covers the technical side of SEO. It has specific steps to optimize your website's HTML code. You should do the first few sections (clusters and keywords.) After that, you can give this section to your webmaster to have these changes made. Anyone with minimal HTML skills can make these changes.

This chapter covers technical SEO. This is based on modifying the HTML in your webpages. In contrast, content-based SEO is based on developing the informational content of your website.

Information Clusters

The search engines identify clusters of information on the web, such as the cluster for cars, the cluster for government, and so on. Search engines then place webpages into those clusters. Porsche webpages are placed in the cars cluster and so on.

- Look at your website's key idea. What is your website about? Search for that general keyword at Google and Yahoo! to find out the cluster where your webpage should fit into. Study the top-ranking pages in that cluster, and then create your webpage (or restructure your website) to match that cluster.

Google will tell you your webpage's category. Search Google for koi. Click the More button and then click Directory. Search for koi once again. In the new results window, at the top, Google lists the category.

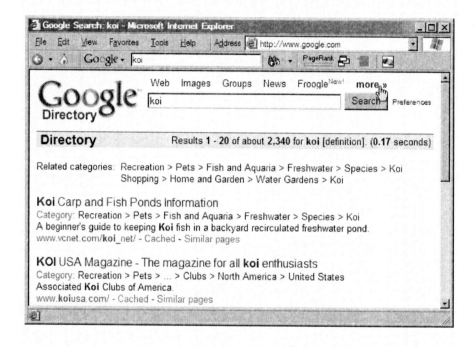

Figure 3: Google shows you the webpage's category. To find this, click More, select Directories, and do another search.

The category will be stated at the top and for each entry. For the first entry, the category is Recreation/Pets/Fish and Aquariums/Freshwater/Species/Koi. For the second entry, the category is Recreation/Pets/Fish and Aquaria/Clubs/North America/United States.

Summary: Make it easy for the search engine to categorize your webpage. Create a webpage that clearly states its theme and purpose. Use Google to find your category, look at the top six to ten webpages in your target category, and build a webpage that matches those.

Relevance Crosslinking: Incoming Links

After the search engine places your page within a cluster, it ranks your page's value in that cluster. Google does this by looking at the number of links to your page from the cluster. If there are lots of links to your page, people in that cluster consider your page to be valuable. If there are few links, your webpage has low value.

So how do you get other pages to link to you? Provide great information at your website and people will link to you on their own. If you write a useful article about how to cure fungus on a koi, dozens of koi owners, aquariums stores, and koi magazines will link to you.

Clusters and incoming links are among the most important concepts in this book. If you do only these two, you'll have great SEO. Create a webpage that is clearly focused on your cluster and add great content that is available for free. The search engines will categorize you in the appropriate cluster, other pages will link to you, and your page will be ranked highly.

You can also get people from related categories to link to you. For your koi website, try to get links from other animal and pet websites, such as cats, dogs, veterinarians, gardening, yard landscaping, and so on.

However, links are not equal. Google ranks a webpage by the quality of the links that point to it. The quality of those links is the logarithmic value of each webpage (the Google PageRank value.) But there's a further complication: the final value depends on the PageRank value of the page divided by the number of links on that page.

- For example, the New York Times has a PageRank 8. The NYT writes an article about your webpage and they include a link to your webpage. This means you get points for having a PageRank 8 page linked to you. However, the final value will be the PageRank divided by the number of links in the article. If the NYT has a list of ten links, the PageRank 8 divided by ten is 0.8 points (this is an illustration.)

- The Montana Koi Ranchers Quarterly has a PageRank 4. They write an article about your webpage, and the link to your page is the only one in their story. The value to your page will be PR4 divided by one = 4.

This means a small article in Montana can give you more points than a big article in the New York Times. It's better to be linked at a page with few links than a page with many links. Ideally, an incoming page should have a few hundred words of text and one link with a relevant keyword that points to your webpage.

 By ranking webpages according to the number of incoming links, Google makes it very difficult for spammers to twist the results, since it's hard to get hundreds of sites to link to you.

- Don't turn away pages with low PR. Your webpage's PR is a total of all pages that link to you. Even small webpages will give you a few points. Dozens of low PR pages will have a higher cumulative result than a few high PR pages. Furthermore, if your PR depends on only a few large PR pages and one of them removes the link to your page, your PR will be affected dramatically. With lots of low PR pages, the loss of a few links will have little effect on your overall PageRank.

- Before you link to a website, check its PR rank. If it has PR-0 (zero) and it has been around for a while, that means Google has blacklisted them. If you link to a "bad neighborhood", you will be penalized. (If a bad page links to you, you won't lose points. Google penalizes you only for what is under your control.)

There are strategies for creating the links within your website. If you crosslink every page to each other, all of your pages will have a low PR because the value is averaged out across all pages. Instead, you can direct the PR value to the most important pages. Add links from the main pages to the minor pages. The minor pages should have links with appropriate keywords to (and only to) the main pages. (The minor pages should not crosslink with each other.) This focuses the PageRank value on the main pages.

If you have good free information at your website, let other websites know about it. Send a summary and a link in an email to the websites within your cluster that have a higher PageRank than your website. Include your main keywords in the link text.

Keywords

A major step in SEOing is to develop the list of keywords that are relevant to your website.

Here's how to come up with a list of keywords:

- Overture's keyword tool: Enter a keyword and it will display related keywords that others have searched. (Don't rely on the numbers from Overture. These appear to be significantly inflated. The actual value is perhaps 2% of what they report.) http://inventory.overture.com.

- Google's keyword tool: Enter a keyword and it will display related keywords. https://AdWords.google.com/select/main?cmd=KeywordSandbox

- Competitor meta-keyword tag: Visit your top five competitors, open their HTML code, and copy their meta-keyword tag. Delete the irrelevant keywords.

- Use stock market analysis tools, such as http://finance.yahoo.com to find analyst reports for your industry. Print these out and highlight the keywords for your industry. (For a quick guide on this, visit andreas.com/faq-research.html.)

- Industry whitepapers: Collect whitepapers and highlight the keywords.

- Industry trade journals: Browse through several back issues of industry trade journals and note the keywords. Look for articles that summarize trends in your industry.

- Log stats: Most web hosting services offer log stats (web traffic statistics.) This shows the traffic to your website. It also shows a list of the search terms that people typed into a search engine to get to your website. Add these keywords to your list.

- Brand names: If you sell Hiromi Koi Pellets, add the product name (Hiromi Koi Pellets) to your keyword list.

- Company names: If you sell Koi Pellets by Hiromi Corp, add the company name (Hiromi Corp) to your keyword list.

Let's develop this list of keywords.

- Use a thesaurus to look for more keywords. The traditional Roget's Thesaurus will show related concepts. Don't use an online or dictionary-style thesaurus. These do not show related concepts.

- Related keywords: Add concepts that are related to your keyword. Goldfish, ornamental fish, and so on.

 You can explore the keywords in the information cluster. Google lets you look at related keywords, synonyms, and so on. To do this, add a tilde ~ in front of the keyword and search at Google. (The squiggle is above the Tab key on your keyboard.) For example, search for ~koi. This shows webpages within the cluster.

- Think about phrases, not words. Most users use two or more keywords when they search. Instead of just koi, add the words Japanese koi fish, koi goldfish pool, koi ornamental pond, and so on.

- Misspelling: Add misspelled versions of the keyword, such as *goldfsih*. Search for *goldfsih* and you'll see how many others have misspelled it.

- Delete irrelevant keywords. Search engines will penalize your site if it has unrelated keywords. For example, if your site is in the koi cluster yet you have keywords such as Britney Spears, the search engines may consider that as a form of spoofing.

- If your site is regional, add regional keywords, such as names of your province, city, valley, and so on. For example, Chicago Koi, Happy Valley Koi, or Tennessee Koi.

- You can also use regional variants and slang. If you're selling crawfish, then these are also called crawdads, crawdaddy, mud bugs, and so on. Use an unabridged dictionary or regional dictionaries to find these words.

- If your website has an international market, then translate the keywords. However, you can't simply convert your keywords from one language into another. For example, house and home are different words in English, but only one word in Spanish (casa). There are plenty of funny examples of translated slogans. You should work with a translator who understands marketing in that language.

The value of an incoming link is based on a combination of the inbound page's PR value and the keywords in that page's link. A page that has lots of keywords and a good PageRank value will rank higher in Google than a page that has a higher PageRank value. For example, search for koi and you'll find the first page is vcnet.com (PR5), the second is coloradokoi.com (PR4) and the sixth site is akca.org (PR6). The highest ranking page (PR6) is ranked lower than the others. Although akca.org has a higher PR, Google calculates that for this search (koi), the other sites were more relevant.

The Keywords in Your Sales Pitch

Now use your keywords to write your sales pitch. This should be a short sentence that uses the top two or three keywords and describes your site's purpose and your product or service.

- Use a short sentence that your grandmother will understand. "Empowering agents to dynamically access the vertical market" doesn't say anything.

- Use complete sentences. Google prefers keywords within a sentence because a sentence has more information.

- The best sales pitch is a spoken phrase, not a written sentence. Try saying the sales pitch to your friends and co-workers. It's good when it doesn't sound awkward.

- To get ideas for your sales pitch, study your top competitors. They probably have written sales pitches for their websites. Read the Google AdWords results for your keyword and look at their websites.

The sales pitch should be more than a short statement (such as We sell koi). It should contain your top two or three keywords, names of specific products or services, and (if relevant) your location. It should also be personal. For example: Koi-Heaven.com is your wholesale distributor of kohaku, showa, and asagi koi in Chicago.

 Looking for ideas on writing your sales pitch? *Phrases that Sell*, by Werz and Germain, is a book with over 5,000 sales phrases in over 80 categories. It also includes two chapters on how to write marketing copy.

Okay, you have your list of keywords and your sales pitch. The next few pages will use these two.

The Website's URL

Use your main keyword to create the website's URL. Search engines look at the words in the URL. Koi-Heaven.com is going to rank higher than Larry-AndJane.com when you search for koi.

 Use a hyphen, not an underscore, in your URL. For example, use koi-heaven, not koi_heaven. Google treats the hyphen as a space and the underscore as a character. This means that koi-heaven will be found if someone searches for koi, heaven, or koi heaven. But koi_heaven will be found only if someone searches for koi_heaven.

- Put your main keyword at the beginning of the URL. Koi-Heaven.com is better than Heaven-for-Koi.com.

- If you already have a URL such as LarryAndJane.com that doesn't match your keyword, then consider changing your current URL. You can set up a redirect on the old site to point to the new site.

 When you print your URL in your advertising, use capital letters to mark the words. It's much easier to read LarryAndJane.com than larryandjane.com.

The Title Tag

The title tag is in the HTML's HEAD section. The code looks like this:

```
<TITLE>Koi and Goldfish at Koi-Heaven.com</TITLE>
```

The title is displayed in the upper left of the browser window. Here's an example of a title tag.

Figure 4: The content of the TITLE tag is shown at the top of the browser.

The title is also used in the description text that appears in the search engine.

Here's an example of titles from Google.

Koi Ponds & Gardens
Welcome to the **Koi**, Ponds & Gardens website. ... You can also find out more about your
local **Koi** club and add your own so that the world knows all about it. ...
www.**koi**mag.co.uk/ - 24k - Cached - Similar pages

Atlanta **Koi** Club: Dedicated to sharing the joy of keeping **Koi**
... Events. Sites to See. Virtual Pond Tour. Vendor Page. Guest Book. Click here for a
listing of all our supporters during the 9th Annual Atlanta **Koi** Show. Webmaster.
www.atlanta**koi**club.com/ - 8k - Mar 29, 2004 - Cached - Similar pages

Figure 5: Google uses the content of the TITLE tag for the headings in the results page.

The TITLE tag's content is what the user sees in the search engine results list.

- Write a good title that will encourage visitors to come to your website.

- When writing the title, use the keyword first and then the name of website. For example, Koi and ornamental goldfish at Koi-Heaven.com.

- Search engines have a limit to the number of characters that they will read from the TITLE tag. This varies according to the search engine, but in general, use no more than 50 characters (this includes spaces).

 To find the number of characters, paste the text into Word and use Tools | Word Count.

The Meta-Description

The meta-description tag also goes in the HEAD section. Here's an example:

```
<meta name="Description" content="A beginner's
guide to keeping koi fish in a backyard pond.">
```

Search engines display the content of the description tag to the visitor in the search engine results page.

Let's look again at those results. Google fetches the content for the two lines of descriptive text from the webpage's meta-description tag. In the following example, the first two are sentences. But the third description is fragments of sentences.

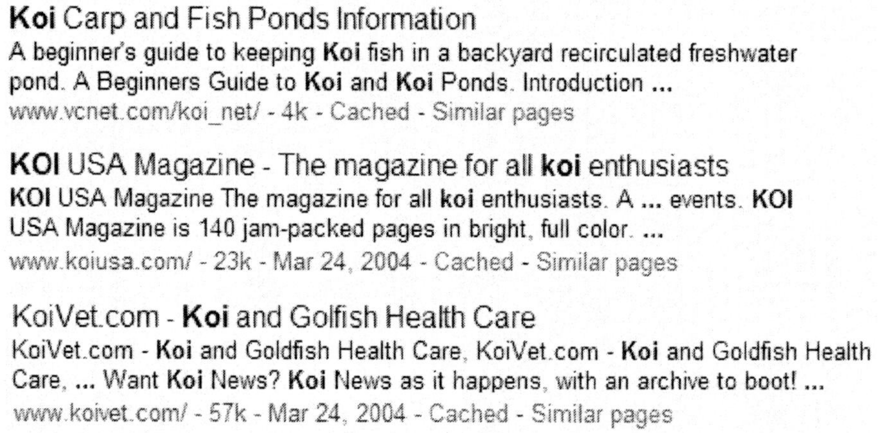

Koi Carp and Fish Ponds Information
A beginner's guide to keeping **Koi** fish in a backyard recirculated freshwater
pond. A Beginners Guide to **Koi** and **Koi** Ponds. Introduction ...
www.vcnet.com/koi_net/ - 4k - Cached - Similar pages

KOI USA Magazine - The magazine for all **koi** enthusiasts
KOI USA Magazine The magazine for all **koi** enthusiasts. A ... events. KOI
USA Magazine is 140 jam-packed pages in bright, full color. ...
www.koiusa.com/ - 23k - Mar 24, 2004 - Cached - Similar pages

KoiVet.com - **Koi** and Golfish Health Care
KoiVet.com - **Koi** and Goldfish Health Care, KoiVet.com - **Koi** and Goldfish Health
Care, ... Want **Koi** News? **Koi** News as it happens, with an archive to boot! ...
www.koivet.com/ - 57k - Mar 24, 2004 - Cached - Similar pages

Figure 6: The third entry is made up of sentence fragments.

The third item has a number of ellipses (three dots). This means that Google isn't using the description tag. Either there isn't a meta-description tag, or for some reason, Google chose to ignore it. Instead, Google's software is fetching text from the body of the webpage. It ignores superlative marketing text, such as "We're the best in the world!" and instead shows sentence fragments that indicate information (such as archive, news, health care, and so on.)

To write your description tag:

- Use your top two or three keywords and write a complete sentence.

- Look at other descriptions in Google and notice what it considers important, such as the words archive, news, health care, and similar.

- Put the keyword first, then the description, and finally the company name. "Keep beautiful Koi and goldfish in your pond. News, FAQ, tips, information, and more at Koi-Heaven.com."

- Use about 250 characters (including spaces). Paste the text into Word and use Tools | Word Count to count the number of characters.

Include your telephone number or location/city/province in the description. Often, people will simply pick up the phone and call. For example: "Keep beautiful Koi and goldfish in your pond. News, FAQ, tips, information, and more at Koi-Heaven.com in Chicago. Call us at 800-KOI-FISH."

Here's how your webpage will appear in the Google listing.

Koi and Goldfish at Koi-Heaven.com
Keep beautiful Japanese **Koi** and goldfish in your pond. News, FAQ, tips, information, and more at Koi-Heaven.com in Chicago. Call us at 800-KOI-FISH. www.koi-heaven.com/ - 23k - Mar 29, 2004 - Cached - Similar pages

Figure 7: Google uses your Title and Description meta-tag text.

Submit Your Description to the Directories

Now that you have the description, submit this to the Yahoo! and DMOZ directories. These lists are edited and maintained by humans. If they think your entry is valuable, they will add it to their directories.

These directories are used by other search engines. The DMOZ file is open source and any search engine can fetch it for free and use it to create their list of webpages.

Since the DMOZ list is edited and evaluated by humans who are experts in those categories, it is considered to be more valuable than lists created by automated indexing tools.

- To submit to DMOZ: http://dmoz.org/add.html
- To submit to Yahoo!: They may charge a fee. http://search.yahoo.com/info/submit.html

Submit as early as possible. Both of these directories can take months to add your site to their lists.

The Meta-Keyword Tag

The meta-keyword tag probably causes the most problems for SEOers.

- The meta-keyword tag tells the search engine what the webpage's main keywords are.

Here's an example:

```
<meta name="keyword" content="koi, goldfish, fish,
ponds, Japanese ornamental fish">
```

Lots of people have heard about this tag, and yes, it was once important, so they insist that SEOers include this tag. However…

- Nearly all of the major search engines ignore the meta-keyword tag because it's too easy to use this to fool the search engines. We wrote about this in the Introduction.

There's also another problem with the meta-keyword tag:

- The meta-keyword tag tells your competitors what your keywords are.

You put all this work into creating the ideal list of keywords and you then place that list in the meta-keyword field. JoesGunsAndKoi.com comes along, copies you, and saves himself an afternoon of work.

Clients always ask us to add the meta-keyword tag. If I tell them it is useless, they think "Ha! I saw this tip on Fox News! Andreas doesn't know anything about SEO!"

So when clients want a meta-keyword tag, we put one in. It's just a few general keywords that don't give away the farm.

And of course, you can look at your competitors' sites and copy their meta-keyword tag into your list of keywords.

 Meta-keyword tags are still used in many intranet search engines. Persons within an organization are unlikely to spoof their own organization's search engine.

File Names

The search engines index the names of files that make up your website. If there are two files named koi-information.html and su-inf.html, you can guess which one will be found when a user searches for koi.

- Use your keywords for your file names. For example, koi-information.html, koi-fungus.html, and so on.

- Use informative names for your files. Avoid cryptic names, acronyms, and so on.

 Use a hyphen, not an underscore, to separate the words in your file names. For example, use koi-heaven, not koi_heaven. Google treats the hyphen as a space and the underscore as a character. This means that koi-heaven will be found if someone searches for koi, heaven, or koi heaven. But koi_heaven will be indexed and found only if someone searches for koi_heaven.

Directory Names

The search engines index the text in the folder names. You can use the folder names to increase your keyword exposure to the search engines. If koi food is one of your keywords, then create a directory with that keyword. For example, Koi-Heaven.com/koi-food/koi-food.html.

If a website has low PageRank, then Google will index only down to a certain depth in the directory tree. As the website gets a higher PageRank, Google will index deeper into the website.

Logo Image

For accessibility of the web by visually impaired users, there is a text= tag in an image. The search engines index the text that is embedded within the link information for an image.

You can put text into that tag and search engines will index it.

```
<img src="images/logo-koi.gif" width="150"
height="100" alt="Keep beautiful Koi and goldfish
in your pond. News, tips, information, and more at
Koi-Heaven.com in Chicago. Call us at 800-KOI-
FISH.">
```

- Add your sales pitch to the alt="" tag in the image link.

- Use the keyword in the image's filename.

- For example, images/logo-koi.gif

We do this only for the logo and banner image. If you want, you can put this text into the alt tag for other images.

Some people will point out that Google has an index of images. Yes, it does, but what it indexes is the text description of the images, not the images itself. No search engine can identify an image. It'd be wonderful if they could index an image: they could identify all the photos of hot housewives and block those pages.

The H1 Header

Okay, now we're getting into the body of the HTML. Here is perhaps the most common SEO error.

- Use an H1 heading on the front page. Google gives emphasis to words in the heading because headings carry information about a page.

Web designers don't like the H1 heading because it's big and ugly. Instead of H1, they use images or body text and modify it with SPAN, DIV, or CSS. That looks nice, but Google wants to see a heading.

By using images or SPAN, the web designer inadvertently undermines the webpage's indexability. Images can't be indexed, so Google won't see those headings. Body text that uses SPAN will be treated as body text, not header text. To get Google to index the heading, use an H1 tag to mark the heading.

- Use the main keyword as the first word in the heading, such as Koi Experts of Chicago.

 You can still have your design. Use CSS to modify the look of the H1 tag so it renders the way you want it. Use <h1 class="whatever"> and then specify the look in the CSS.

The Body Paragraph

The body text is the text on the front page. This text should be descriptive, informational, and have lots of keywords.

- Put your main keyword at the beginning of the body text.
- Repeat the main keyword several times within the first 25 words.
- Work the other keywords into the body text.
- Repeat the main keyword at the end of the front page.
- Use complete sentences in your text.

- Avoid phrases such as "Best in the World!" Some search engines ignore these phrases.

- Use words that mark information, such as news, guide, and summary.

 If you use emphasis such as bold or italics, Google considers that to be additional information. Put a few of your keywords in bold or italics.

- Google also offers Local Results. If a user adds a city name into a search, the user will see a list of relevant businesses and services in her city. If your location is relevant to your product or service, add your city, telephone number, and zip code to your front page.

Figure 8: Google's Local Results will display webpages in a city.

If your products or services are regional, you can make sure that your website is added to Google's Local Results. Send a short email with a description of your business or service to local-listings@google.com.

Hyperlinks

The search engines give more attention to the text in hyperlinks, since these take effort to create and hyperlinks often point to information.

- Put the keywords in the hyperlink. Example: Read <a href=http://www.koi-heaven.com/koi-fungus.html>how to cure fungus in koi</a>.
- On the first page, add links that point to your informational pages.
- Note that the file has an informative and relevant file name.

Site Maps

Some websites uses JavaScript or roll-down menus for the navigation. However, some search engines ignore JavaScript and thus won't follow the links at your site. There is the same problem with site maps that use images.

- Create a plain text site map that lists all of the webpages. Place a plain text link to the site map on the index page.

Validate the HTML

Some search engines pay attention to the quality of your HTML. One of the differences between amateur and professional websites is whether the HTML is written correctly.

- Write clean HTML code.
- Use HTML validation software to make sure your code is compliant to the current standards.

Several More Items for Websites

Here's a few general methods for dealing with your website's ranking in search engines.

Update Your Website Every Few Weeks

Remember the two billion webpages that are ignored because they've been abandoned? If you don't make changes to your website, the search engines may conclude it is no longer active.

 Every few weeks, add a news item, a review, or a new item to your website. Update the front page. The search engines will give you a higher ranking. Google will also index your website more frequently if you get a higher ranking.

If you're wondering how to tell when Google has indexed your site, there's a way to find out. If Google has recently indexed your site, it adds the date of indexing to the results page. These are called fresh tags. In the following illustration, which was created in early April 2004, we see that Google indexed the second webpage on March 29th, 2004.

Google indexes the web generally in the last week of the month. Webpages with high Google PageRank are indexed more frequently.

- If you have changes, be sure to add them by the 20th of the month so they'll be indexed.

Koi Ponds & Gardens
Welcome to the **Koi**, Ponds & Gardens website. ... You can also find out more about your local **Koi** club and add your own so that the world knows all about it. ...
www.**koi**mag.co.uk/ - 24k - Cached - Similar pages

Atlanta **Koi** Club: Dedicated to sharing the joy of keeping **Koi**
... Events. Sites to See. Virtual Pond Tour. Vendor Page. Guest Book. Click here for a listing of all our supporters during the 9th Annual Atlanta **Koi** Show. Webmaster.
www.atlanta**koi**club.com/ - 8k - Mar 29, 2004 - Cached - Similar pages

Figure 9: Google's Fresh Tags (the date after the URL) show when the second website was reindexed.

Add a Blog to Your Website

Blogs are a great way to quickly add content to your site. Just open a text box, type your entry, click Submit, and you're done.

To learn more about blogs, see the blog FAQ. It discusses blogs and the various types of tools. The FAQ is at CreativeConsultantsGroup.com/seo

If you want a free, quick-and-easy blog, then use blogger.com. If you want a better blog, you'll need one of the commercial blog tools. We've tested all of these; the best one is movable-type.org.

Web Traffic Analysis

Your website keeps track of every action. All of this information is recorded in web traffic logs. You use log analysis programs to display this information in charts and tables. Traffic analysis lets you see:

- Which pages are popular or not. This tells you where to invest more effort, or which pages to delete.

- How users came to your site. It will list the pages from where they came. You can contact those websites and suggest link exchanges.

- The websites that your visitors are hopping to. Again, you can contact those sites and suggest link exchanges.

- Which search engines are sending traffic to your website. You can increase your efforts at those search engines and reduce expenses at ineffective search engines.

- The keywords that users use when they search for your site. You can add those words to your keyword collection and develop additional material. You can delete ineffective words.

Keep the Search Engines Out

In some cases, you may not want a search engine to index your webpage. Perhaps you have pages that are not relevant to the public.

There are two ways to keep search engines out of your site: the robots.txt file and the robots meta tag.

The robots.txt file is a file with a list of files which should not be indexed by a search engine. Create a text file, add a list of files, save it as robots.txt, and place the file in the main HTML directory where your index file resides.

```
User-agent: *
Disallow: /cgi-bin/sources
Disallow: /access_stats
Disallow: /cafeteria/lunch_menus/
```

There is also the robots meta tag. This is a tag that is placed in the head tag of each webpage to be excluded.

```
<META NAME="ROBOTS" CONTENT="NOINDEX, NOFOLLOW">
```

The NOINDEX means it should not index the page. NOFOLLOW means it should not follow any links from the page.

Just because you use this doesn't mean the page won't be indexed. There are hundreds of search engines and not all of them follow this.

The Main Search Engines

We could write a long list with descriptions of each search engine, but what really matters is simple:

- If you are targeting the US market, you have to be in Google (about 65% of all searches are done on Google or Google-powered search engines), Yahoo! (about 15%), and MSN (about 15%). The remaining 5% doesn't matter. (For statistics on search engine market share, see searchengine-watch.com/reports.)

- You also need to be in the directories. Because the directories are built and edited by humans, they are considered reliable. The content of directories are used by many search engines for their indexes. The two main directories are Yahoo! and DMOZ.

 There are also specialty search engines. If your market is large enough that there is a portal or search engine for it, then investigate those search engines and learn how to get your site listed.

Outsource the SEO

Finally, if you don't want to spend your days at tweaking code and following the latest changes in search engines, you can outsource the entire project to SEO services. Just search for SEO in a search engine.

SEO Problems

The rest of this chapter covers a few things that cause problems for your website and search engines.

Informational Pages, Doorway Pages, Portal Sites

In order to drive traffic to a commercial site, the webmaster may create additional websites with general information that concludes "And more for, visit OurRealWebSite.com".

These pages are called informational sites, doorway pages, cookie cutter sites, or portal sites.

- These offer no informational value to users. Directories (Yahoo! and DMOZ) ignore these sites. Search engines may blacklist these sites.

Flash, Graphics, Frames, Passwords, and Broken Links

- Web designers and graphics designers love Flash, because it allows them to create beautiful websites. For example, see one9ine.com. However, search engines cannot index Flash. The site looks great, but it will not be listed in search engines.

- Don't create a website that uses only images. Some designers do this to use unique fonts. It looks nice, but search engines can't read images and won't index them.

- Websites from the mid-90s use frames. Many search engines can't index the content of frames. If your website uses frames, rebuild it so it doesn't use frames.

- Pages behind a password will not be indexed. If there is content that you want to have indexed, then copy it to a non-secured page.

- If a link is broken, the search engine can't follow it. Use link validation software to test the links.

There's also automated submission. "Pay $10 and have your website submitted to 600 Search Engines!" You don't have to submit your website at all. If your website has good information, others in your cluster will link to your website and the search engines will find you.

Spammer Techniques

Search engines use tools to look for these tricks. They will blacklist your website if you use spammer tricks.

- Link farms are pages that have dozens or hundreds of links. Spammer sites use these to bury their links among hundreds of valid links. Avoid link farms.

- Spammers use Meta-Refresh to misdirect visitors. You search for Britney Spears and go to a website named AllAboutBritneySpears.com where you realize in shock that you been redirected to a website about Justin Timberlake. This is done by using an instant refresh. Search engines will penalize for instant refresh. If you use meta-refresh tags, set this to five seconds or more.

- Cloaking and stealth scripts are used to mislead the search engines. To the search engine, it shows one website (all about Britney Spears), but to the visitor, it shows a different website (Justin Timberlake.)

There are more spammer tricks, such as duplicate pages, keyword stuffing, fake pages that are not related to the website's real content, and keywords hidden with background colors. Don't use these or you'll be blacklisted.

How Search Engines Deal with Spammers

If a website is using spammer tricks, the website's ranking will be lowered or the website, including the IP address, will blacklisted.

If one of your competitors is using spammer tricks, report them to the search engine to have them removed. Send an email to:

- spamreport@google.com

- spamcrusader@inktomi.com

Summary: Search engines know about these SEO tips and tricks. For example, Google uses the H1 Header to evaluate a webpage. But if this is abused too much, they may stop using this. But what they really want to index (and it's also very hard to spoof) is information. So make these SEO changes to your website, but put your real efforts in providing informational content.

SEO Checklist for Your Website

The following page is an SEO checklist for your website.

- Photocopy the page and check off the items. The items in the checklist are explained in this chapter through examples, notes, and tips.

Done	Item	Description
	Information Clusters	Create a website that is clearly focused on your category's information cluster. The search engines will categorize you in the appropriate cluster.
	Keywords	Develop your keywords. See the keywords section.
	Sales Pitch	Use your main keywords to write your sales pitch. Write a short sentence that describes your site, your product, your service.
	The URL	Put the keyword at the start of your website's URL.
	Title Tag	Put your sales pitch in the TITLE tag. Not more than 50 characters. Search engines display the content of the TITLE tag in the results page.
	Meta-Description	Put your sales pitch in the meta-description tag. Not more than 250 characters. Search engines display the content of the DESCRIPTION tag in the results page.
	Submit to Directories	Submit your sales pitch to Yahoo! and DMOZ.
	Meta-Keywords	Put only a few keywords in the meta-keyword tag.
	File Names	Use your keywords for your file names. For example, koi-information.html, koi-fungus.html, and so on.
	Logo File Name	Use the keyword in the logo image's filename. For example, images/logo-koi.gif
	Logo Image ALT Tag	Put your sales pitch in the logo image's ALT tag.
	Headings	Use an H1 heading tag on the front page. Use CSS to modify the look of the header. Use the main keyword as the first word in the heading
	Body Text	Put the main keyword at the beginning of the body text. Repeat several times within the first 25 words. Use complete sentences. Include your sales pitch. Put a few of your keywords in bold or italics.
	Hyperlinks	Put the keywords in the hyperlink. Example: Read <a href=http://www.koi-heaven.com/koi-fungus.html>how to cure fungus in koi</a>.
	Site Map	Create a plain text site map that lists all of the webpages. Place a plain text link to it on the index page.
	Validate the Code	Use validation tools to check the HTML and links.

Pay Per Click and Your Website

In this Chapter

This chapter covers the Pay Per Click (PPC) services, which allow you to pay to be listed in a search engine. There are two major PPC services: Google AdWords and Overture. This chapter discusses Google AdWords in detail, along with strategies and tips for managing your Google AdWords account.

 PPC isn't really SEO, but this service is generally managed by SEO companies because it relies on many of the same SEO methods, such as keywords.

Use Pay per Click to Get to the Top

There is another way to get ranked highly in search engines. This can put you at the top of a search engine nearly instantly. Pay Per Click, also called Paid Placement, is a paid advertising service that place your ad on a search engine.

- In SEO, you tweak the HTML and hope that the search engine will index your webpages. You also hope the search engine will use your carefully crafted sales pitch. But you have very little control over the results.

- In PPC, you pay to play. You have complete control over the text to be displayed. Placement is based on how much you pay: the more you pay, the higher your ad will be placed.

PPC generally means using the Google AdWords and Overture ad placement services. At both of these services, you place a bid and your ad is displayed according to the other bids within the same category.

What Is PPC?

First, let's look at an AdWord. In the following illustration at the right side of the Google results page under Sponsored Links, there are three ads. These have a heading, two lines of text, and a URL.

These are paid ads from three different koi companies. If you click one of these, you will go to that company's website. When you click, Google charges that company a fee for the click. If the company bids 25¢, then Google charges 25¢ for the click. (We'll explain the details later.)

Google displays only eight ads per page. If you go to the second page, you'll see eight more ads.

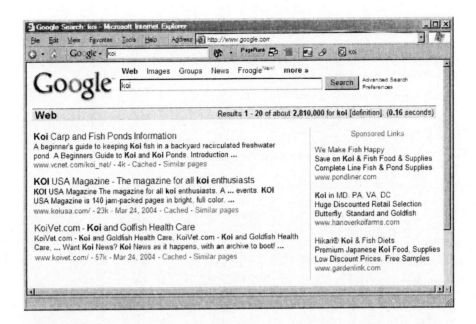

Figure 10: The AdWords ads are displayed in the right column under Sponsored Links.

How PPC Works

Here's what happens when you sign up for an AdWords account at Google.

- You create a small AdWords button. The AdWord has a title, two lines of text, and the URL.

- You add a list of keywords. When visitors at Google search for these, your ad is displayed. If a visitor clicks your ad, your website comes up.

- You set the daily maximum for your budget. If you set this at $2, then Google will display your ads until you reach $2 in clicks and then it stops for the day. Google spreads the ads across the day, so you won't use up your entire budget in the morning.

- Depending on what you bid for that particular keyword, Google will charge your account for the click. If you bid 12¢, Google charges you 12¢ for the click .(We will explain the details below.)

- The account is linked to your credit card. When Google bills you, they deduct it directly from your credit card.

- AdWords has elaborate reporting tools that shows you the number of clicks, the percentage of views vs. clicks, the cost per click, your ad's average position, and whether the visitor was converted to buying.

There are more details, but you'll learn this when you start using AdWords.

The Drawbacks of PPC

First, let's look at the drawbacks of PPC:

- PPC is quick and easy. Depending on the size of your credit card, you can be at the top of the page at Google within 15 minutes.

- PPC can be expensive. If the category is crowded, others will bid competitively for the top spots.

- PPC is a temporary solution. In a long-term strategy, PPC does not get a webpage into the core of the web. It does not add the webpage to a community. If you rely on PPC, you will forget how search engines work and your website will not be in the core of your category.

- SEO companies prefer PPC because they can charge a commission for this service.

- Old-school marketing prefers PPC because this is the way they've been selling advertising for decades. Did TV ads produce any results? Who cares? They got their commission.

- Companies prefer PPC because they are accustomed to paying for services. They assume that paid services (Business Class) are better than free services. By paying, they get control over ads, text, and placement.

All of these conspire to raise the costs of PPC. Companies will easily spend tens of thousands of dollars on PPC without checking the effectiveness of the PPC campaigns.

The Benefits of PPC

There are very good reasons to use PPC.

- You pay, you play. You can get the top positions at the search engines.

- Most competitors don't use PPC, so you get placement above them. Although there are 2.9 million koi webpages, you can be listed at the top with a relatively small ad budget. With careful bid management, you can get great results for very little money.

- Google AdWords has very good tracking and reports. You can see what works and fix what doesn't work.

- PPC really works. AdWords bring traffic. You can track this in the AdWords statistics.

We've seen this over and over in nearly every field: there's very little competition. Only a fraction of companies are using AdWords. There are some 13 million registered companies in the USA. Only about 200,000 advertisers are using AdWords at Google (Business Week, April 2004).

When you start working with AdWords and look at your competitors in your market space, you'll notice most of those AdWord campaigns are not effective. Google is secretive about AdWords and their help pages are not very helpful. If you design a good ecommerce strategy which includes AdWords, you should be able to improve traffic and revenues.

Let the Market Decide

With AdWords, every action can be tracked. There are detailed statistics for everything that happens with your ads.

- When you create the ads, you should create not just one or two ads. Create 12-15 ads. Don't worry too much over what goes into the ad. Try all sorts of variations and ideas. Try flippant ads, silly ads, and flat ads.

- Run the ads for a week or so and look at the results. The ads will be sorted by click rates and you'll see exactly how each ad works. For whatever reason, people will click on ad #5, but they'll ignore ad #2. The market will tell you which one is best.

This is a problem for ad agencies. They bring in someone with 20 years of experience to write your ads. Or you get an intern to make twelve ads with different texts, random stuff, try this and that. Which one does a better job?

Google AdWords will show you what the market actually prefers. Just create the ads, throw it out to the masses, and see what they go for.

It's always surprising which ad is the winner. You can't predict this in advance. It's also surprising that there can be a large difference in response rate to ads with nearly the same words.

- It's hard to sit down and create 12 different ads. We've found it works best if you don't think about it. Just create all sorts of variations. In one ad, put line A and B, in the next ad, reverse them. Mix up the words.

Someone could probably write a text randomizer that lets you type your keywords and it adds a bunch of sales lines and mixes it up.

 Stuck for ideas on writing your AdWords? There's a useful little book with lists of marketing phrases. Phrases that Sell, by Werz and Germain, has over 5,000 phrases divided into some 80 categories. It also includes two chapters on how to write marketing copy.

- AdWords is Darwin's Survival of the Fittest in action. Create at least twelve ads and see which produces a higher Click-Through-Rate (CTR). Delete the weak ads. If an ad works, don't change it. Create variations of the successful ads and see which ones work.

- Run the campaign for at least 1000 impressions. You need about that many ad views to draw a meaningful conclusion. Delete the weak ads and create more.

Google displays AdWords to users when the ad's keywords matches the user's search terms. Google also displays ads to users when the ad's keywords are related to the user's search terms. For example, if the user searches for tennis shoes, Google will offer ads for tennis shoes. This is an example of Google's CIRCA technology, which is able to match terms that are relevant, related, or in the same category. This means when you are coming up with your list of keywords, you should think of related concepts, terms, synonyms, and so on. Try as many keywords as possible. Use your Adwords account to delete the words that don't produce traffic.

Problems to Avoid

- In the first week or two, Google's grammar patrol will complain about your ads. They are very picky. When they send you a notice that your ad doesn't meet their guidelines, just modify the ads.

- Do not add dozens of keywords at once. This will lead to a low average CTR and Google will turn off the ad.

- Don't forget logarithmic distribution of page views. The large majority of users see only the first page. Your AdWord should ideally be in the top three positions.

- Marketing departments are accustomed to $50,000 ad campaigns and they will power bid to get the #1 spot. The max is $20 per click, but there's no maximum on the daily cap. If you get into a bidding war for the #1 spot, it can get very expensive. Position #2 or #3 are just as visible to the users and these are cheaper.

The Daily Cap isn't a solid number. If you cap your budget at $20 per day, you might end up paying slightly more on some days. Google may adjust this up or down during the month, but all in all, you won't pay more than $20/day for the number of days in that month. In January, this can be $620 (31 days) and in February it can be $560 (at 28 days). This isn't much of a difference, but it can become significant for clients with $500 daily budgets. Depending to the number of days in a month, their monthly costs can range from $14,000 to $15,500.

AdWords Acronyms

Google adds yet more acronyms. Here's an explanation.

Acronym	Explanation
Clicks	Every time someone clicks on your AdWord, that's one click.
Impr	Impression. When the Adword is displayed to someone, that's an impression. It doesn't mean they saw it. They had the opportunity to see it. Just as when you're browsing through a magazine and there is an advertisement for a Honda, that's an impression.
CTR	Click Through Rate. This is the number of people who clicked on the ad, compared to the number of impressions. The CTR is stated as a percentage. If the AdWord was displayed 100 times and 25 people clicked it, then that's a 25% CTR.
CPC	Cost Per Click. This is what you bid to pay for each click. However, the actual amount will be lower. This is explained in the section Adjusting the Bids.
Avg CPC	The average Cost Per Click. Based on a daily average of the CPCs. If this is significantly lower than your CPC bid, then you should adjust your bids.
Cost	The total that you're paying for that AdWord. This is the number of clicks multiplied by the actual CPC.
Conv. Rate	If you set up Conversion Tracking (strongly recommended) then this column reports on the percentage of visitors who bought a product.
Cost/Conv	This shows the total costs of your campaign against each click. If the overall Cost was $12 for 50 clicks and you made two sales, both of those sales cost you $6 each in advertising. This is the most significant number on the page: your Cost/Conv should be within the range that you're willing to pay for advertising the product. If this number is greater than your profits, then you're losing money on the sale.

That last item needs a bit more explanation. Let's say we're selling offspring from our award-winning koi. To raise Koi-san, it takes 25 pounds of koi food pellets, 2,000 gallons of bottled Japanese spring water, and so on. We add that up and it costs $50 for one year. We decide to sell the koi for $100. Our profit margin will be $50. Therefore we should be willing to spend a percentage of that profit on advertising the koi. How much? If we allocate $25 in advertising (in other words, another cost), we end up with a $25 profit. If we spend $60 per koi in advertising, we've lost money on the koi.

Remarkably, many people set their advertising budget on a guess. "Oh, $500/month sounds about right." With AdWords, you can see the effectiveness of a campaign, which lets you justify the advertising budget. If the advertising is effective, that is, if it produces revenues and profit, then you can increase the budget.

To set an initial advertising budget, calculate the advertising cost per item that you're willing to spend (how much you're willing to spend to make one sale), the number of sales you expect to make each month, and then work backwards to set the monthly budget, the daily budget, and the bid price. After a month of results, you can look at the conversion tracking and adjust the budget.

AdWords can do more than just sell products. You can use Ad-Words to create mailing lists. Write the AdWords with text such as Free Newsletter and point this to your newsletter signup page. If you are preparing a product and the release date is months away, you can already start by building a mailing list of potential customers.

Writing the Ads

- Use your list of keywords (see the section on keywords in the chapter on Technical SEO). Use the keywords for the title and body text.

- Use capitalization in the URL. Instead of writing koi-heaven.com, use Koi-Heaven.com. This is easier to read.

- Look at the AdWords of your top competitors. Print out their ads and use their text to get ideas to create new ads.

- If appropriate, include your price in the ad. This deters unqualified buyers. If you write that koi are $500 each, buyers who are looking for $1 koi will go elsewhere. You save money if they don't click on your ad.

- Use phrases that invoke positive emotions. Examples: Free, cheap, sale, tricks, you, tips, fact, learn, discover, free shipping, fast, easy, convenient, best, sexy, quick, fun, instantly, save time, powerful, save money, most popular.

- Use phrases with a call-to-action. Examples: Buy today, save 50%, download free trial now, sale ends tomorrow, sale-priced, special offer, limited offer, and similar.

- Negative ads which evoke fear or worry are not as effective as positive ads. Negative phrases include: avoid, worried about…, bankruptcy, don't get caught… and so on.

- Don't mislead. Users strongly dislike deceptive or misleading links that get them to click on a link. They will instantly back out and return to the search engine. For more, see the Consumers Union study mentioned in the Introduction.

Search for popular, expensive items and look at the AdWords for ideas on how to write your AdWords. Those AdWords were probably written by ad agencies. For examples of well-written ads, search for cruise vacations, jewelry, and so on.

AdWords Matching

There are several ways to enter the keywords. You can add quotation marks around the words, use square brackets, or nothing at all. Here's an explanation from Google for each one.

- **Broad match**. Enter your keywords, such as tennis shoes. Your ad will show when users search on tennis and shoes, in any order, even if the query includes other terms, such as tennis rackets and running shoes. Google also uses expanded matching. This means Google will use other relevant terms and variations (such as tennis sneakers).

- **Phrase match**. Place quotes around your keyword "tennis shoes". Your ad shows when users search for tennis shoes in that order and with other search terms. For example, your ad will show for red tennis shoes but not the phrase shoes for tennis.

- **Exact match**. Place brackets around your keyword [tennis shoes] Your ad will show when users search for tennis shoes in this order without other terms. For example, your ad won't show for the queries red tennis shoes or tennis bags and shoes.

- **Negative keyword**. Include a dash before your keywords, such as -red. If your keyword phrase is tennis shoes and your negative keyword is -red, your ad will not show if a user searches for red tennis shoes.

Setting the Initial Bid

Google will suggest a bid and a daily budget, but these are just guesses from Google. They have no idea of your sales volume or advertising margins.

 Estimate how many units you will sell in one month and then use your advertising margin to calculate the monthly advertising budget. Use this to set the daily budget. Set the bid to 5¢ and then adjust upwards to get into the top three positions.

For example, we expect to sell 50 koi at $100 each per month. We're willing to pay $10 to advertise each koi, so that's a monthly advertising budget of $500 ($10 per koi for fifty koi). Divide $500 by 30 days and that's $16.66 dollars per day. So we set the daily budget at $16.66. Now we adjust the bids to get our AdWords at the top of the list.

Adjusting the Bids

The major task in AdWords is to adjust your bids to keep your costs down and your ad position up.

- Your ad should be in the first five ads on the first page for your category. Due to logarithmic numbers, traffic falls very fast after the first page.

The bid price is not a simple number. The actual amount you'll pay depends on the bids from other advertisers.

Let's say there are only three companies with AdWords in the koi market. Apple bids $15, Berry bids $10 and Cherry bids 5¢.

- The actual price each company will pay is 1¢ plus the next lowest bid.

The best way to explain this is with an example. Laura clicks on all three ads. What does each company pay for that click? Start at the bottom of the table and work up.

Company	They Bid	They Really Pay	Why They Pay That Amount
Apple	$15.00	$10.01	Apple pays the next lowest bid (Berry's $10 bid) plus 1¢. Apple pays $10.01.
Berry	$10.00	$00.06	Berry pays the next lowest bid (Cherry's 5¢ bid) plus 1¢, so Berry pays 6¢.
Cherry	$00.05	$00.05	Cherry bid 5¢, so he pays 5¢.

If you look carefully, you'll see Ms. Berry and Mr. Cherry are paying pennies for their ads, but Mr. Apple is paying $10.01 for his ad.

- You can wildly overpay if you don't manage your bids.

 If you misunderstand this bidding system, your campaign can be severely affected. If both Apple and Berry have a $20 daily budget, Apple will get only two AdWords displays ($20 divided by $10 = 2), but Berry will get 330 displays ($20 divided by 6¢ = 330). Although Ms. Berry and Mr. Cherry are bidding less than Mr. Apple, they will sell more koi.

- To adjust the keyword's bid price, log into your account and enter the AdGroup.

- Look at the table of keywords. At the far right, it lists the Avg Pos (Average Position.) This is the position where your ads are showing up. The keyword ornamental goldfish is at 7.9, which means it is usually #8. You want this to be at #3 or so.

- Click Edit Keywords.

- The textbox Edit Keywords and CPC displays your keywords. For example, it lists the keywords:
  koi fish
  ornamental goldfish
  koi supplies

- At the line ornamental goldfish, add a double asterisk and the amount of your bid. For example, type **0.51 (fifty-one cents) after ornamental goldfish. The list will then look like this:
  koi fish
  ornamental goldfish**0.51
  koi supplies

- Click Estimate Traffic to see where Google estimates this will appear. If it went up to only position 5.5, then you'll need to increase the bid.

- Type ornamental goldfish**0.76 and click Estimate Traffic again. Continue to raise the bid until it reaches #3.

 People tend to think in increments that match US coins. They bid 5¢, 10¢, 25¢, 50¢, and so on. You can often beat the others by offering one cent above the increments. Bid 51¢ instead of 50¢.

AdGroups

One of the challenges of Google AdWords is the multiple levels of Campaigns/AdGroups/ AdWords. It takes some time to become familiar with this. Some people create dozens of campaigns, with a single AdWord in each campaign. Others put all the Adwords within the same AdGroup.

When you enter into your Google AdWord account, you click on a campaign. This brings you down to the AdGroup level. You click on an AdGroup and this brings you down to the AdWord level.

Category	Description	Example
Campaign	Use this level to create various campaigns and set the overall daily maximum for each campaign. For example, you can set the maximum at $10 per day for a campaign.	If you're selling different products, then create a campaign for each product. The Koi-Campaign for koi and the Turtle-Campaign for turtles.
AdGroup	Within the campaign, you create AdGroups. Each AdGroup can be for a sub-product.	For the koi, there would be Red-Koi-AdGroup, the White-Koi-AdGroup, and so on.
AdWord	Within each AdGroup, you create several AdWords. This is a group of keywords that will trigger any of the Adwords ads. You should create at least nine ads for the set.	The keywords will include koi, ornamental fish, and so on.

- Use the Campaigns to control the overall spending for a product line.

- Create different AdGroups. Each AdGroup contains the products within that group.

- Within the AdGroup, create the AdWords.

For example, you sell koi and you also offer repair services: roof repair and plumbing. Create two campaigns: one for koi and the second for repairs. Within the first, create four AdGroups for the four kinds of koi that you raise. Within the second, create two AdGroups, one for each service. This lets you control the costs for each campaign.

Strategic Bidding

Bidding is actually quite fun. It's like playing poker with your competitors. You bid 50¢. They raise their bid to $1. You raise your bid to $1.25. It's a game of bluff and one-up. But there are also several tricks to this.

- You can find what your competitors are bidding. Enter your AdGroup and click Edit Keywords. In the text box, you'll see a list of your keywords.

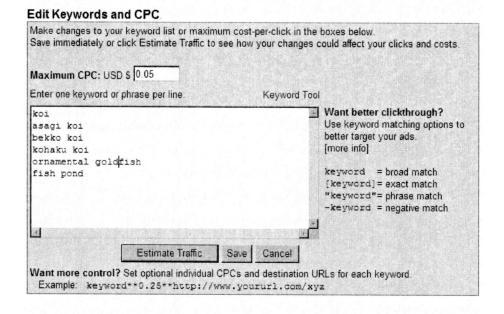

Figure 11: The Edit Keywords page lets you adjust the bidding for each keyword.

Insider's Guide to SEO

- Click on Estimate Traffic. In the new page, the following table appears. Let's go through these items.

Keywords	Clicks/Day		Avg CPC		Cost/Day		Avg Pos	
	current	forecast	current	forecast	current	forecast	current	forecast
asagi koi	< 0.1	< 0.1	$0.05	$0.05	$0.00	$0.00	1.0	1.0
fish pond	0.1	0.1	$0.05	$0.05	$0.01	$0.01	4.2	4.2
koi	2.7	2.7	$0.05	$0.05	$0.14	$0.14	3.6	3.6

Figure 12: The Estimate Traffic table shows Google's estimates for the traffic.

Clicks/Day	The estimated clicks per day. This shows the current number (if you already have this word in a campaign) and the forecast. For the word koi, there will be 2.7 clicks per day, or about 80 per month (2.7 x 30).
Avg. CPC	Average Cost Per Click. This shows the current and forecast CPC. The current is what you currently are bidding. The forecast is what you enter in order to see an estimate. In this example, these are currently at 5¢.
Cost/Day	The cost per day, both current and projected. For the word koi, it will cost 14¢ per day at 5¢ per bid.
Avg. Pos.	Average Position. This is where Google estimates your ad will appear in the list of ads. For Asagi koi, it will take the #1 position. The phrase fish pond however will be at position 4.2. To raise it to a higher position, you increase the bid. The word koi will also be at position 3.6.

If you can afford to bid for position #1, then do that. Otherwise, aim for position two or three. In this case, we increase the bids for fish pond and koi.

- In the Edit Keyword text box, add **0.51 after the words. That's two asterisks and the bid price (51¢.) Click Re-estimate Traffic.

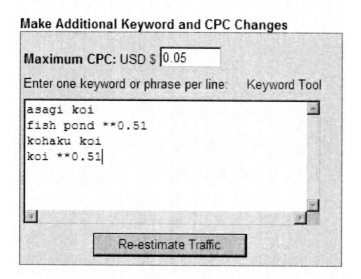

Make Additional Keyword and CPC Changes

Maximum CPC: USD $ `0.05`

Enter one keyword or phrase per line: Keyword Tool

```
asagi koi
fish pond **0.51
kohaku koi
koi **0.51|
```

[Re-estimate Traffic]

Figure 13: Set the bid for a word by adding two asterisks and the bid price.

When you click Re-estimate Traffic, Google will recalculate the costs per day (for koi, that would be 2.7 clicks at 51¢ = $1.35 per day or about $40/month.)

Sometimes, Google will present a new estimated position at 0.0. Either the keyword has such little traffic that Google can't estimate a rank for it, or it's a Google error. If this happens, click Re-estimate Traffic again (perhaps several times) until it displays a number, such as 2.4.

If you get 1.0, it means you have the highest bid and your AdWord will be #1. However, you'll probably be overpaying. Your competitors in the action-filled world of competitive koi breeding will be bidding less than you but they will display more ads.

Reduce your bid by half and click Re-estimate Traffic. Continue to adjust your bid until you have the ad at the position you want. If you want to be #1, then bid just enough to beat the others. This can often be only a few cents. It is just as good to be in position #2 or #3 and you'll save quite a bit.

For our example with koi, we checked the actual bids for koi at AdWords. It turns out that 5¢ gets position #3.6, but raising it to a mere 6¢ will buy position #1. One cent makes the difference. Apparently none of the other koi breeders have realized that.

 Generally, you should set your AdWords account to show the statistics for the last seven days.

If your market is very competitive with lots of bids, there's a way to find the optimal number. Bid very high (for example, $20) and then reduce the bid by half several times. Go from $20 to $10.01 to $5.01 to $2.51 to $1.26 and so on. At $20, your ad will be #1. Adjust the numbers by half each time until you see the ad drop from #1 to #2. If it drops in position when you change the bid from $5.01 to $2.51, then try the number halfway between those two.

By trying the halfway number over and over, you can quickly find the tipping point that causes your AdWord to drop in position and thus find out what your competitors are bidding.

Let's look at the example of Apple, Berry, and Cherry one last time. Ms. Berry spends a bit of time to find out what her competitors are bidding. She notices that Mr. Apple is overbidding. Ms. Berry could raise her bids to just under Apple's bid. She still pays Cherry's bid plus one cent. However, Mr. Apple would be paying Ms. Berry's bid price plus one cent. For example, if Ms. Berry raises her bid to $14, she would force Mr. Apple to pay $14.01 for his ads and she is still paying only 6¢. By forcing Apple to overpay, she maxes out his daily budget and removes him from the competition. And you thought koi breeding was just a quiet Zen hobby.

 We've noticed that many people create a single AdWord, set their bids, and never touch it again. You can tell if someone has only one AdWord. Look at the Google results page and press Refresh (or the F5 key) several times. If they have different ads, Google Adwords will cycle through the various ads and display these. If they have only one ad, it will repeat, over and over. This is bad for your competitor, it means he isn't testing his ads to see which one is effective and deleting the ineffective ads. Very likely, he is also not paying attention to his bids. Of course, you shouldn't interfere with the gentleman's style of playing poker.

PPC Strategies

The visitor is searching for a product. She took the initiative to type in the words into a search engine. She chose to click on your AdWord. When she comes to your webpage, you immediately show her what she is looking for. She doesn't want to read your website's front page. She wants to buy a koi now.

The landing page must be highly relevant to the user's search. If the landing page is not relevant, she will go to the next website.

- The AdWord should point to a landing page that is tailored to the ad. You must create a landing page with relevant information that will convert the customer. The URL may read Koi-Heaven.com, but when they click, it'll send them to koi-heaven.com/buy-koi.html where there is a photo, a description, and a Buy Now button.

- Create specific ads for each product. If you're selling Koromo koi (a breed of koi), then create an AdGroup just for Koromo koi, put koromo in your keyword list and advertisement, and then point the ad to a unique landing page, such as koi-heaven.com/buy-koromo-koi.html, where the visitor sees a photo of a Koromo, reads about Koromo, and can fill out his name and credit card information on the same page.

- The landing page has to allow a short and simple transaction. The longer the page and the more steps, the more buyers you will lose.

- Review the ads every day for the first twenty-one days and every week after that.

- Aim for a 1% (or higher) click-through-rate. If you're not getting at least this level, adjust your campaigns.

- In Edit Settings, select the regions, countries, and languages. Don't advertise your product or service outside of the appropriate region or language. You'll only pay for useless clicks.

This strategy moves the emphasis away from the website. For the last ten years, the focus was on websites as a set of pages with information about the products, pages about the company, help pages, contact pages, and so on. Graphics designers built websites as a consistent set of pages. This approach was based on the company's perception of itself, or the graphic designer's concept of a unified message.

- However, as we've seen, search engines don't index websites. They index webpages. For the purpose of ranking highly in a search engine, the emphasis should be on creating an informationally valuable webpage and getting other webpages to link to it.

- The user who is looking to buy a product or service is not searching for a website. She is looking for that particular product or service because it fits her needs. The webpage should be customer-centric. What is the customer's need? How does the webpage fulfill that need?

If the landing page is customer-centric, most customers will arrive, find their need is fulfilled, and they will buy. A few customers want to look around and for them, the website should include the usual pages about the company, background, answers, and so on. The emphasis, however, should be on the customer.

You can set up an AdWords campaign ahead of time and have it ready to start on the product release date. Create the campaign, select the keywords, write the ads, and then put the campaign on Pause. This turns off the campaign. On the morning of product launch, remove the pause the campaign. To pause a campaign, select the AdGroup and click Pause.

AdWords are nearly instantaneous. When you turn these on, people will see them within minutes. In comparison, it can take weeks or even months for a website to get highly ranked.

We built a website for a client who was about to release a new $65,000 enterprise software product. While we were building and testing the website, we prepared the Adwords campaign and put it on pause. When everything was tested and finally ready, we turned on the AdWords campaign. Within 45 minutes, he had his first request for a product demonstration.

When preparing a product release, you may need to consider the various time zones. If you're rolling out a product for the US market, the advertising should be available at 9 AM in New York City.

Content Targeting at AdSense

Google has an affiliate program called AdSense. People sign up and Google displays Adwords on their webpages, where the webpage is related to the search terms. When visitors click on an ad, Google gives part of the click fee to the sponsor website.

For example, someone is looking at a koi website. On the side of the page, the Google AdWords are listed, including your AdWord. The visitor clicks on the AdWord to learn more about your koi. You pay a click fee to Google, and Google gives part of that to the website.

To see an example, go to aquarist-classifieds.co.uk and notice the AdWords at the right side.

The problem with content targeting is that visitors didn't necessarily arrive at that page by searching, so they are not highly motivated. You will pay for those clicks anyway.

- You should experiment with Content Targeting. If it works for your website, then it's okay. If not, turn it off.

- To turn off Content Targeting, go to Edit Settings in your AdWords account.

Content Targeting at Gmail

Gmail, Google's free email, similar to Hotmail and Yahoo! free email accounts, is another way for Google to increase the display of AdWords.

Google will look for keywords in emails and then insert related advertising into the email. For example, you write to your friends about plans to go bass fishing. Gmail will insert Google AdWords advertising that are related to bass fishing.

Gmail includes Google search, so when people search their emails, another Google AdWord will be displayed.

AdWords Conversions

One of the best features in AdWords is the conversion tracking. A click on your ad is nice, but what really counts is when the visitor buys your product. This is a conversion from visitor to buyer.

From the dotcom crash, we learned that traffic is irrelevant. Who cares if you have 16 million visitors? The only thing that counts on an ecommerce site is sales.

AdWords offers a free conversion tracking tool. You fetch a bit of HTML code at AdWords and place it in your website's thank-you page. This is the page that a customer sees when they have finished making a purchase. This lets AdWords know that the visitor clicked on the AdWord, came to your site, and bought the product.

The conversion tracking shows the number of conversions, the percentage, and the total cost per conversion.

You can also track the lead generation. If you use the website to capture names for your mailing list, the conversion tracking will show the number of leads, the effectiveness of the lead conversion, and the total costs of the lead generation campaign.

- To set up Conversion Tracking, click on it in the AdWords toolbar.

- You can select Basic or Customized. Basic will track a conversion. Customized tracking will let you distinguish between conversions for leads, sales, signup, or page views. Select the one you want.

- In the final page, Conversion Tracking will ask for the security level of the conversion page. The conversion page is the thank-you page that the customer sees when she has signed up for a newsletter or made a purchase. Google tracks this page because that's proof that the viewer was converted from a visitor to a customer. Conversion pages are usually HTTPS (note the S at the end) because these are secured sites. Some conversion pages, especially for newsletter signups, are unsecured HTTP pages. If you're not certain, visit your thank-you page and look at the URL in the browser bar. Select the appropriate type. The page will refresh itself and the HTML code will be displayed in a text box.

- Copy the conversion code. We suggest that you save it in a Notepad TXT file (do not save this in Word, which may insert formatting and break the code.)

- Paste the code in the HTML at the bottom of your thank-you page. When your customers sign up for a newsletter or make a purchase, they may notice the following Google tag on the conversion page.

Google™ Site Stats
Send feedback

Figure 14: The AdWords Conversion tag appears on the thank-you page.

> Set up the conversion tracking when you create the campaign. This lets you keep good statistics about your campaign.

AdWords Reports

AdWords includes a powerful reporting tool. This lets you keep track of your campaigns. You can create reports to show the effectiveness of your ads, the results, and the conversion rates.

You can also set up Reports to send a report to you every week or every day. You should use this at the start of every campaign.

If anything, the Reports tool has too many features. We only use part of it. Here's a quick guide to using Reports.

Log into your Adwords account and select the Reports tab. In the following illustrations, we've trimmed the images for clarity.

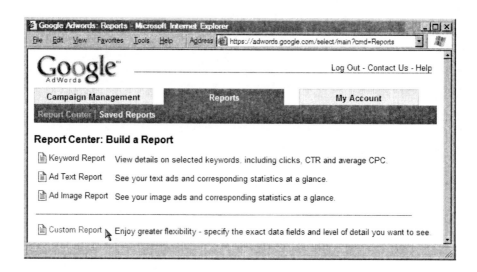

Figure 15: To set up a custom report, select Custom Reports.

At the bottom of the page, select Custom Report. This brings you to a new page where you design your custom report. This lets you select the items.

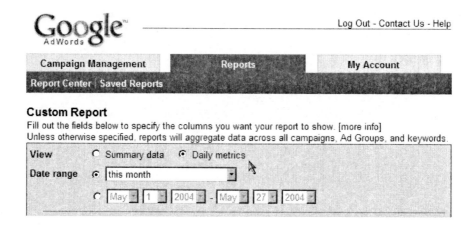

Figure 16: Select Daily metrics.

Custom Reports lets you generate a graph so you can see the trends. The following steps show how to do this.

Select Daily Metrics and then use the dropdown menu to select the date range, such as This Month or Last Seven Days. Generally, you should select a time period with at least one thousand clicks. If you select less, the data won't be indicative of the general trend and the results may be misleading.

Scroll to the bottom of the page and select Graph. From the dropdown menu, select the information that you want to see in the graph, such as Impressions (how many people saw the ad), CTR (Click-Thru-Rate), or similar.

Graph   ☑ Include graph of Impressions ▼ * only for daily metrics, view online

Format   ⦿ View online (.html)   ○ Downloadable (.csv)

Save and email   ☐ Save this report as [   ]

and email it to me as an attachment | never ▼ | *

[Create report]   [Clear form]

Figure 17: Select Graph and then select the type of information for the graph.

After a few moments, AdWords Reports will generate a graph for you.

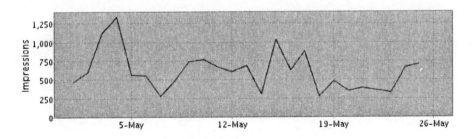

Figure 18: An example of a graph for impressions.

The above graph shows the number of impressions for our ads. This graph shows a whole month, and you can see the general cycle for the weeks. The impressions peak at the middle of the week on Tuesday and Wednesdays and drop on the weekends. Employers are right in their suspicions: the workers are goofing off and cruising the web. The graph helps you to see the effect of campaigns on your traffic.

Here's another graph. This shows the average position of the ads.

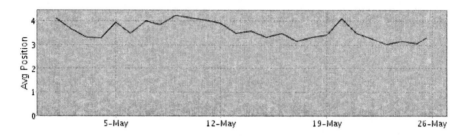

Figure 19: An example of a graph for Avg Position (average position).

In this case, the ads are in position 3 to 4. Since we want the ads to be in position two or three, this is acceptable. If we increase the bids slightly, we can bring the ads into position two. If the ads are in position 4, 5, or lower, that's a bad sign because of log scales and the traffic will fall dramatically. If the ads are in position 1, we may be overbidding on the ads.

Here's another graph.

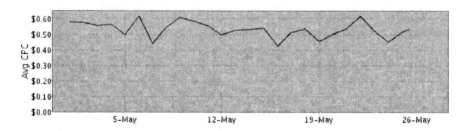

Figure 20: An example of a graph for Avg CPC (average cost per click).

This graph shows the average Cost Per Click (CPC). For this campaign, we're paying between 50¢ and 60¢ per click. There are no large changes. This means the competitors aren't making much changes to the bids.

Let's try another graph. This shows CTR (Click Thru Rate). This is the number of people who click on an AdWord.

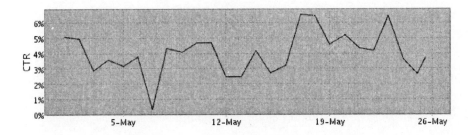

Figure 21: An example of a graph for CTR (Click Thru Rate).

In the CTR graph, the range is mostly between 2% and 5%, with a few peaks at 6% and a dip to 0.5% on the 7th of May or so. This is acceptable. The CTRs should stay above 1.5% or so.

Conflict of Interest: The Media Buy

PPC creates a conflict of interest between the client and the SEO company. In traditional marketing, the ad agency sets their fee on a percentage of the media buy. If the client buys $100,000 worth of advertising in TV media, then the ad agency charges, for example, 30% as its commission, which would be $30,000.

This means that the more the client spends, the more the agency gets. There is little incentive for the agency to convince the client to buy less, in fact, it would be against the agency's interests. Any employee who tells a client to spend less money will be soon looking for a new job.

- The tracking and reporting tools in PPC offers a solution. Instead of basing the fee on a percentage of money spent, agencies should charge a percentage of the revenues generated by the ad campaign. This gives the agency an incentive to improve the campaign: the better the results, the more they earn.

Overture's Bid Service

The first bid PPC service was Overture. It is widely used among SEO companies. However, we don't use it for several reasons:

- Overture does not use search relevancy. Your ads are displayed regardless of relevancy. This will lead to more clicks but less conversion.

- Overture doesn't penalize underperforming ads. If your ads aren't performing well in Google AdWords, they will shut off your account. In a way, that's annoying, but Google also obligates you to improve your campaign. Both you and Google earn more.

Overture places your links into search engines such as AltaVista, Go.com, Infospace.com, IWon.com, MSN, and Yahoo!. The first four search engines have low market share. At MSN, it's difficult to tell the difference between paid links and search engine results. Considering the reactions from users in the Consumers Union report and studies that show that users only look at the first ten links, it's not too promising.

But who knows? Go ahead and try it. You might get better results.

 We are constantly learning more about AdWords. For updates, visit our website at CreativeConsultantsGroup.com/seo.

Summary: PPC works and you should use it. However, PPC is an expensive solution that distracts from the goal. The overall best strategy is to identify your webpage's information cluster, build a theme site, and add lots of information-rich content. This delivers better results (highly motivated customers) and your webpages will be ranked highly by the search engines.

Content-based SEO

In this Chapter

This chapter covers content-based SEO, which is developing the informational content of your website.

Content-based SEO is the key strategy to getting your website identified in the proper category and ranked highly. Content-based SEO will give you much better long-term results than technical SEO.

Content-based SEO or Technical SEO?

So what is the best SEO strategy? Technical or content? Modify the HTML code or add ten articles to your website?

- In the introduction, we wrote that 85% of searches are for information. In order to have the highest number of users, the search engines compete with each other to offer the best results, which means the best information for each search.

- Google wants to see useful information. This means information that is so good that other sites link to it. So add information to your site, get other sites to link to you, and Google will rank you higher.

- If you do only technical SEO by modifying the HTML code, your site will be at risk of falling in the rankings. Search engines don't like it when people use tricks to modify their ranking. If a method is being abused too much, the search engines will block that method. The websites that were based on that trick will fall off the charts.

Google changed their search engine in late 2003 and early 2004 to improve the ranking of informational webpages. The rankings for webpages by universities, colleges, magazines, and dissertations went up. Sites with something for sale slid down in ranking.

Adding Content

Many corporate sites are actually very small. They have perhaps 15- 20 pages. There just simply isn't very much there to be indexed.

- You should plan to add at least 25 to 50 pages of content. Ideally, you should have several hundred pages. This is not unrealistic: my personal website andreas.com has over 500 files.

- These articles can be about your company, your products, your services, your industry, the history of your industry, overviews of the industry, stories about customers and clients, trends, projections, reviews, analysis, and so on.

- These articles should be customer-centric. It should be information that your customers want to see, not just marketing text. Don't just offer your product. Explain how to cure fungus on koi. Describe the home remedies. If it is useful information, other sites will link to it.

- These don't need to be long articles. Each article can be one or two pages.

Use SEO on the Content

When you write these articles, don't forget to use your SEO skills. Weave your list of keywords, your sales pitch, and other information into the texts. The articles should be rich in keywords so the search engines can easily identify the appropriate cluster and then index your pages.

Insider's Guide to SEO

Get keyword list (handwritten)

- Give your keyword list to your writers and ask them to use these words in the article.

- Use H1 heading tags in the heading of each article and put keywords into the headings.

- Add emphasis (bold and italics) to several of your main keywords. If a word is emphasized, Google assumes it has more informational value.

- Add links to the articles and include your keywords in the link text. Instead of writing "Click **here to read more**", write "More on **Organic Food for Koi**".

Hire a Writer

To get articles for your website, you can hire professional writers and journalists. You can either let the writer put her name as the author of the articles or often, the writer will agree that you can put the CEO's name as the author of the articles. Just as the speeches of CEOs are usually written by professional writers, the articles by CEOs and CTOs at many websites are written by professional writers.

- Contact industry magazines and trade journals and ask their editors if they can suggest a writer for your project. Often one of the staff writers will write the articles for you, either under his name or an assumed name.

- Hire writers from the NWU. Their members include 3,500 professional business writers and technical writers who write articles for hundreds of business magazines. See nwu-resumebank.com and nwu.org/hotline.

- Ask your fans to write articles. If there are people who are passionate about your products or industry, ask them to write articles.

Learn More about Marketing on the Web

There are several resources for ecommerce marketing:

- Dr. Ralph Wilson's website is one of the best-known resources for marketing on the web. He has hands-on reviews of tools, such as e-newsletter managers, ecommerce software, and so on. Visit his website at WilsonWeb.com.

- Mitchell Levy was at SUN Microsystems, where he managed the e-commerce for Sun's $3 billion supply chain. He wrote the book E-Volve-or-Die.com. His website is a great resource on ecommerce. Visit his website at ECnow.com

- Rodney Rumford tears Adwords apart. His book has a number of valuable tips and ideas. TheInfoGuru.com/Google_Adwords_Expert.htm ($39 for a PDF).

Distribute Your Content

Now that you have your content, don't be shy with it. Encourage other websites to link to it. The more links to your website within your information cluster, the higher you will ranked on the search engines.

 Write a short description of the article, include a link to your article, and send an email to websites in your category. Be sure to put your main keywords in the link text. Invite them to link to your website.

Conclusions

Most SEO books, articles, companies and services are based on technical SEO. They tweak the HTML code to take advantage of how the search engines index the webpages.

There are several problems with technical SEO. As we have explained in this book, most searches are done by users who are looking for information. Search engines want to deliver relevant results, which means they want to deliver the best information on a topic. Search engines don't like it when websites use techniques that fool the search engines because that lowers the quality of the results. If this gets out of hand, the users will abandon the search engine. Therefore search engines are on the lookout for SEO techniques and they counteract those.

Technical SEO has a deeper problem. If you do only technical SEO, you will concentrate your efforts on a technical fix. You will forget that the search engines are looking for information. If you don't create solid information, you won't be placed in an informational cluster, others won't link to you, and you won't be ranked highly. Technical SEO by its nature can not help you with this.

The PPC services, such as AdWords and Overture, are useful and they work, but they should not be the central strategy for your website. Once again, you'll concentrate on adjusting the bids and you'll forget about the information clusters.

- Both of these methods will lead you to spending time on tweaking code and chasing numbers. You will forget to pay attention to the logarithmic nature of the web, network theory, and the goal of search engines.

The best long-term SEO strategy is what we call content-based SEO. This takes advantage of the nature of the web, namely, logarithmic power laws and network theory. This also plays into link relevancy, where search engines are competing with each other.

- Create a website that has a clear theme that fits into your information cluster. Add lots of good information. Other websites will link to your website. Your website will become significant within your cluster.

- Due to logarithmic power laws, your website will get the large majority of the traffic in your market cluster.

- Due to preferential linking, your website will remain significant in its category.

- To improve their search relevancy, the search engines look for the websites with the best information. Search engines evaluate your webpages according to the number and quality of links from your cluster.

Now you understand Google's reply to the question "How should I SEO my website?" Google said "Write good content." Yes, but Google didn't explain the background for that answer. Now you know.

Definitions and Acronyms

When you deal with SEO people, they'll use lots of acronyms. Here's a list of the most common terms.

Term	Definition
Anchor Text	The text in the clickable part of a URL. For example, in the link <a href=http://www.koi-heaven.com>Visit Koi-Heaven.com</a>, the "Visit Koi-Heaven" part is the anchor text.
CPC	Cost per Click. The fee for a click. More about this in the section Pay per Click. See also PPC.
CTR	Click Through Rate. The rate of clicks on a link. If your website's advertisement is displayed six times and two people click, then that's a 33% CTR (2/6=33%).
DB	Database.
DMOZ	Directory at Mozilla, or The Open Directory Project (ODP) at Mozilla. This is a human-edited volunteer project to create a directory of the web. The DMOZ directory is open-source and many search engines use it as content for their database. Pronounced DEE-Moss. Visit DMOZ.org.
Informational Content	Information for visitors at a website, such as articles, FAQs, help pages, and so on.
IP Address	Internet Protocol Address. The numeric address for a URL. For example, Koi-Heaven.com's IP address is 204.332.104.57. See also URL.

KW	Keyword. What someone enters in a search engine to search for something. In practice, this means key phrase, which is several keywords.
Links	In network theory, a link connects nodes to other nodes. For the web, links connect pages to other pages.
Natural Search	SEO companies use this term to distinguish PPC (paid placement) from unpaid placement. They mean by this that the company did not pay to be listed in the search engine and it somehow happened naturally. They also call this organic search.
Node	In network theory, a node is the point which has links to other nodes. For the web, nodes are the webpages.
ODP	Open Directory Project. An open source project by volunteer editors to create a human-edited directory of the web. Also called DMOZ.
PPC	Pay Per Click. Services such as Google AdWords and Overture which place your ad in exchange for payment.
SE	Search Engine. SEOers usually abbreviate this as SE. Two examples of SEs are Google and AltaVista.
SEM	Search Engine Marketing deals with placement in both search engines (using SEO) and PPC, such as Google AdWords.
SEO	Search Engine Optimization. A method of tweaking a webpage's HTML code so it ranks higher in a search engine. Among SEO people, this is also a verb (We SEOed the website) and a person (She is our SEOer.)
SEP	Search Engine Promotion. Improving your website's position in search engines. This is another word for SEO.
SERP	Search Engine Results Page. This is the position that your webpage gets in a search engine. For example, if your webpage is at position #7, then your page is number seven in the SERPs.
Spamming a Search Engine	Trying to place your websites in as many categories as possible on a search engine.
Spoof	Trying to fool or mislead a search engine. SEO is basically spoofing the search engines.
Tweaking	To make changes and modifications, as in tweaking the code. Technical SEO is basically tweaking the HTML code.
URL	Universal Resource Locator. The text address for a website. For example, Koi-Heaven.com. See also IP Address.

SEO Tools of the Trade

SEO companies use a number of tools. Here are some of the significant ones.

WebPosition Gold (WPG)

WebPosition Gold (WPG) analyzes the text in the top websites in your category. It then gives you a report so you can modify your website to match those sites in keyword weight, frequency, word count, and so on. WPG is the basic tool of SEO companies.

Be careful with WPG. You can set it up to automatically check your position at search engines and automate submissions to search engines. The search engines don't like this, because it leads to tens of thousands of queries. If they find you are using this, your website may be blacklisted.

Link Swap Management

Link swap management tools find potential crosslink partners, ranks the websites, sends email to them, keeps track of requests, and checks to see if the partners maintain the crosslinks. Here are several tools:

- optitext.com/optilink
- arelis.co.uk
- linkpopularitycheck.com
- addme.com/linkwatch.htm

- acceleratedsoftware.net/linkexchangemanager.html
- linksmanager.com/features.html

 Be careful with these link management tools. Google recognizes if you're using some of these and will ignore your links.

Find Your Website's Rank on the Web

Alexa.com lets you find how where you rank on the web and whether your website is rising or falling.

Go to alexa.com and enter your URL. In the results page, click See Traffic Details. We find that koi.com is #340,438 on the web (out of six billion, so that's quite good.) It also shows koi.com moved up 175,000 places in the last three months.

 Alexa's Traffic Rank numbers are not the actual traffic numbers for those sites. It uses statistics from Amazon and Alexa, which only shows what they report. Nevertheless, Alexa gives you an idea of a website's relative popularity compared to other websites, such as your competitors. For example, if your site's Traffic Rank is 100,000 and your competitor is 200,000, then your site is roughly twice as high. It doesn't mean that you're actually number 100,000.

See How Much of Your Website Is Indexed

This tool shows how much of your website is indexed at Google/AOL, Alltheweb, AltaVista, HotBot, and Inktomi.

If your website has 200 pages, this tool may show that only seventeen of the pages are indexed. The search engines don't know about the remaining 183 pages at your site.

- Go to marketleap.com/siteindex and select Search Engine Saturation. You can also see how your competitors are doing. Type their URLs in as well. Type the three-letter password that appears at the left side of the screen (the case doesn't matter) and press Enter.

- If the search engines aren't indexing your 183 webpages, you can easily fix that. Create a site map and place a link to it on your index page. The next time the search engines index your site, they will find the sitemap and add the missing pages.

To See What Google Indexed at your Website

You can see a list of the pages that Google has indexed at your website.

- Go to Google and search for site:koi-heaven.com

- If Google hasn't indexed your webpages, create a site map and place a link to it on your index page. Google will find it and add the missing pages.

HTML Validation and Link Analysis

You need to test your HTML to make sure it is correct and matches the current standards. Use the code validation in Allaire HomeSite, Macromedia Dreamweaver, or other professional tools.

- The W3C has a free validator at http://validator.w3.org

Overview of Search Engines

Danny Sullivan's searchenginewatch.com is a useful website for information about search engine technologies and features:

- searchenginewatch.com

- searchenginewatch.com/webmasters/features.html

- http://searchenginewatch.internet.com/links/Major_Search_Engines/The_Major_Search_Engines/

SEO Websites, Newsletters, and Chatlists

There are a number of SEO resources. You can also use these to find someone to SEO your website.

- SearchEngineWatch.com

- WebMasterWorld.com

- IHelpYouServices.com/forums

- SearchEngineForums.com

- Seochat.com

- Sewatch.com

- SearchEngine-News.com

- Axandra's newsletter: join-search-engine-facts@list.netatlantic.com

SEO Associations

There are also several SEO associations. You can find someone to SEO your website.

- Sempro.org

- Webmasterworld.org

 For more on web marketing, there's Thomas Wong's book *101 Ways to Boost Your Web Traffic: Internet Marketing Made Easier*. More at intesync.com.

References

Here are books and articles cited in this book. You can find a list of clickable links at CreativeConsultantsGroup.com/seo

- Study on how users understand search engines by Consumer WebWatch at consumerwebwatch.org/news/searchengines/index.html.

- The Pew Research Center has a number of studies on web usage. For a study on search usage, see pewinternet.org/reports/toc.asp?Report=80 and pewinternet.org/reports/toc.asp?Report=64

- Study of Excite searches shows that users look at only the first pages. See jimjansen.tripod.com/academic/pubs/jasist2001/jasist2001.html

- For tips on writing your sales pitch or AdWords, see Phrases that Sell, by Werz and Germain.

- A good resource for ecommerce is at Mitchell Levy's ECnow.com.

- Study by Pennsylvania State University on business searches at Excite. Summary at firstmonday.dk/issues/issue6_7/spink

- For more on bibliometrics and cybermetrics, see the journal of Cybermetrics at cindoc.csic.es/cybermetrics/. There is also Don Turnbull's article on bibliometrics and cybermetrics at ischool.utexas.edu/~donturn/research/bibweb.html.

- For more on logarithmic power laws, see Narushige Shiode and Michael Batty's article at isoc.org/inet2000/cdproceedings/2a/2a_2.htm

- Network theory is discussed by Albert-Laszlo Barabasi in *Linked: The New Science of Networks* (2002). His website is at www.nd.edu/~alb/

- Origins of Google in *The Anatomy of a Large-Scale Hypertextual Web Search Engine,* by Brin and Page at www-db.stanford.edu/~backrub/google.html and *The PageRank Citation Ranking: Bringing Order to the Web,* by Page, Brin, Motwani, and Winograd at http://dbpubs.stanford.edu:8090/pub/1999-66

- There are number of good articles about PageRank. See Ian Roger's article at iprcom.com/papers/pagerank, Andrew Gerhart's article at searchengineguide.com/orbidex/2002/0207_orb1.html, Harjot Kaleka's article at searchguild.com/article112.html, Tony Bury's article at sitepoint.com/article/999?, and Phil Craven's article at webworkshop.net/pagerank.html

- IBM Almaden Research Center's paper on the distribution of the web at almaden.ibm.com/cs/k53/www9.final/

Index

Notes

Notes

Notes

Insider's Guide to SEO